The Equitable, dedicated to serving our clients for over 125 years, is pleased to provide this free copy of the comprehensive book, *The Price Waterhouse Guide To The New Tax Law*. Whether for personal or business needs, you'll find everything you need to know about the new tax laws between these covers.

Your local Equitable representative is another valuable resource when planning for the future. To locate the Equitable office nearest you, refer to the handy directory in the back pages of this book.

THE EQUITABLE

A Financial Services Company of Distinction

The Equitable Life, founded in 1859, has a long history of helping individuals and businesses provide for their future financial security. Originally founded to serve life and health insurance needs, today The Equitable and its subsidiaries, offer a full range of financial services.

- Equitable protects over 30 million Americans with life, health, annuity and pension coverage.
- Equitable's assets under management total over $100 billion.
- Equitable is the third largest life insurance company and institutional investor in the U.S.
- Equitable has continually pioneered new and innovative forms of insurance protection.
- Equitable is one of the country's largest investors of capital for financing—homes, farms, apartment houses, commercial buildings, job-creating enterprises and more.

Let The Equitable Financial Companies help you plan for a secure financial future.

THE PRICE WATERHOUSE
GUIDE TO
THE NEW TAX LAW

Introduction by
Roscoe L. Egger, Jr.
Former IRS Commissioner

PREMIUM EDITION

BANTAM BOOKS
TORONTO • NEW YORK • LONDON • SYDNEY • AUCKLAND

THE PRICE WATERHOUSE GUIDE TO THE NEW TAX LAW
A Bantam Book
Bantam edition / October 1986

ISBN 0-553-26590-3

Published simultaneously in the United States and Canada

Bantam Books are published by Bantam Books, Inc. Its trademark, consisting of the words "Bantam Books" and the portrayal of a rooster, is Registered in U.S. Patent and Trademark Office and in other countries. Marca Registrada. Bantam Books, Inc., 666 Fifth Avenue, New York, New York 10103.

PRINTED IN THE UNITED STATES OF AMERICA

O   20 19 18 17 16 15 14 13 12 11

CONTENTS

INTRODUCTION

BY ROSCOE L. EGGER, JR.

The Tax Reform Act of 1986 is the most significant and comprehensive tax legislation passed since the beginning of World War II. The provisions included in this legislation will have a considerable effect on every individual and business in this country for many years to come.

This new law reflects the chief objective of its framers: Those with similar incomes should pay essentially the same amount of taxes. This injects an element of fairness into the system that has been absent from prior tax laws. At the same time, the new law reflects a sharp departure from the recent trend toward attempting to cure a wide variety of social and economic problems through tax incentives, or perhaps more accurately, tax subsidies.

In attempting to achieve these results over the past several decades, exclusions, deductions, and credits that provide special exceptions for all sorts of activities have been added to the tax code. For example, in order to encourage investment in equipment and plant modernization, Congress in the early sixties approved the investment tax credit and accelerated depreciation.

Business has not been the only beneficiary of the special tax rules popularly known as "loopholes." Individuals have been urged to save and invest through "all-savers" certificates. Special tax treatment has been granted to dividends, interest, and contributions to retirement plans. Taxpayers have been encouraged to use credit through the allowance of unlimited deductions for interest paid on home mortgages and consumer debt of every kind.

These tax benefits and many others have offered ways for Americans to lower taxable income and, thus, tax liability. They have also resulted in a tax code riddled with myriad exceptions and benefits for a host of special-interest groups. Although these tax benefits were initiated with the best of intentions, they produced a code that was extraordinarily complex. More importantly, they had the singular effect of reducing the tax base, thus shifting the burden of providing needed federal revenues to an ever-narrowing constituency.

The advantages that taxpayers secured through tax preferences gradually became a powerful incentive to base investment decisions primarily on tax consequences. This in turn created distortions in the investment decision-making process as well as a perception of unfairness in the system.

In 1984, while I was Commissioner of Internal Revenue, we conducted a public opinion survey regarding existing tax laws. Among the conclusions:

• About four out of five taxpayers in the country believed that the tax system benefited the rich and was unfair to the ordinary working man or woman.

• About three out of four taxpayers believed their income taxes were much too high.

• The majority of taxpayers believed that a large percentage of the public cheated to some degree on their taxes. In fact, about one in five of those surveyed actually admitted cheating on their own taxes.

In addition, over the years there have been new allegations that many of the nation's largest corporations have avoided taxes because of special rules crafted especially for them. The same charges have been leveled at high-income individuals who, using a variety of income-sheltering techniques, have reduced their tax bills in many cases to little or nothing.

The message was unmistakable: The vast majority of Americans believed they were carrying a disproportionate share of the tax burden. This perception clearly had a serious undermining effect on our tax system, with troubling implications for the future. For if the tax system is to provide needed federal revenues, we must rely heavily on voluntary compliance. And we have seen that the public perception of tax inequity has had a damaging effect on that compliance.

In recent years there has been rapid growth in the "underground economy," or as it has more accurately been described, the "tax gap"—the difference between what taxpayers should be paying in income taxes and what they do in fact pay. As a result the revenue shortage has reached staggering proportions. In studies recently completed by the Internal Revenue Service, the tax gap for 1986 is estimated at $103 billion. This compares to about $39 billion just ten years ago. Many believe that this phenomenon can be attributed in part to a growing disenchantment with the system.

In determining how to approach tax reform, then, one of the principal goals was to find a way to ensure that all individuals and corporations would pay a fair share of the tax burden, regardless of the tax incentives available to them. Another objective was that the law be as understandable and as straightforward as possible, to avoid manipulation of statutory complexities that works to the advantage of the sophisticated and the disadvantage of the financially naive.

Certainly, for individuals with more complex returns, and for much of the business community, the objective of simplification has not been met. But the Tax Reform Act of 1986 does go a long way toward simplification for many individual taxpayers. To begin with, it drops over six million low-income taxpayers off the tax rolls and reduces the number of individuals who need to itemize deductions. Additionally, the lowering of rates should go far in eliminating the incentives for taxpayers to construct complicated tax shelters.

The new tax code will combine significantly lower rates for individuals and businesses, with a tax base that is expanded through the repeal or modification of many of the incentives initially designed to encourage social or economic goals. This code will treat all taxpayers more fairly: Under the new rules, it will be virtually impossible for any profitable company or wealthy individual to avoid paying tax.

It is no doubt true that changes will be made over the coming years to address unforeseen inequities or problems in the new law. But in my view the Tax Reform Act of 1986 represents the most significant step toward true tax reform in this generation. Its pluses far outnumber its minuses.

In designing the new program, both the Administration and Congress have adhered to their major goals of tax equity and simplification. Millions of individual taxpayers will benefit from the lower rates, increased standard deductions, and personal exemptions, as well as modifications of confusing tax provisions.

For many of us, however, and certainly for businesses, simplification is virtually impossible due to two major factors:

1. We no longer live in a world of simple business and financial transactions.

2. The dramatic changes in the tax rules themselves present complexities.

Simplicity and fairness cannot always exist side by side. In my judgment, Congress and the Administration have correctly chosen fairness over simplicity in many of the provisions of the tax reform bill. All taxpayers—individuals, corporations, and other entities—now face complicated new rules under the Tax Reform Act of 1986. That is an inevitable and necessary transition from how it used to be to how it should be.

This book describes in plain English key features of the new law. I hope it will shed light on the new rules as they apply to you, and simplify the task of applying them in your particular circumstances.

Roscoe L. Egger, Jr. served as Commissioner of the IRS from 1981 to 1986 and is now with Price Waterhouse.

THE PRICE WATERHOUSE GUIDE TO
THE NEW TAX LAW

PART 1
WHAT THE NEW TAX LAW MEANS TO YOU

CHAPTER 1

THE 28 PERCENT SOLUTION
How the Tax Rate Cuts Affect Your Bottom Line

CHANGES AT A GLANCE

Old Law	New Law
Fifteen brackets, ranging up to 50 percent	1987: Five brackets, ranging up to 38.5 percent
	1988: Two brackets, 15 and 28 percent
Taxpayers may use income-averaging	Income-averaging is no longer allowed
Two-earner deduction is available to working couples	Two-earner deduction is eliminated
Taxpayers may exclude $100 of dividend income from taxation	Dividend exclusion is no longer permitted

It should come as no surprise that much of the ballyhooed Tax Reform Act of 1986 is not what it appears to be.

Granted, some taxpayers will pay less under the new system. But a substantial number of Americans will pay the same amount or more.

Why? The new law is chock-full of provisions that diminish the tax savings of the new, vaunted two-bracket tax structure.

Specifically, the curtailment or elimination of many popular tax deductions will put a larger chunk of your income within Uncle Sam's reach.

The result: Lower rates may produce—for many individuals and businesses—only the illusion of sharply lower tax bills.

Like a funhouse mirror, the new law can make your personal tax burden seem lighter without its having shed a single pound.

THE TWO-BRACKET SHUFFLE   Taxpayers who find themselves paying more under the new tax system will be particularly hard hit in 1987. The Tax Reform Act mandates that the new structure be gradually phased in over 1987. But let's look first at how the system will work when it becomes fully operational for tax years beginning after 1987.

As in the past, the amount of tax you pay depends on your filing status—single, head of household, married filing jointly, and so on.

Under the new law there are only two tax brackets—15 percent and 28 percent. The 15-percent rate applies to income equal to or below:

• Married individuals filing joint returns and surviving spouses	$29,750
• Heads of household	$23,900
• Single individuals	$17,850
• Married individuals filing separate returns	$14,875

Income in excess of these amounts is taxed at the rate of 28 percent. These amounts will be adjusted for inflation for tax years beginning after 1988.

Say you're married, file a joint return, and your taxable income—after deductions—adds up to $50,000 in calendar year 1988. Under the new system you'll pay total taxes of $10,132.50 when you sign your return in 1989. Here's how your tax bill adds up:

• First $29,750 of taxable income at 15 percent	= $4,462.50
• Remaining $20,250 at 28 percent	= $5,670.00
	$10,132.50

What could be simpler—and fairer?

But remember, we're talking about 1988, when most of the tax reform package is in place. It's a different story in 1987.

In this first year of reform, most taxpayers will find the tax bite larger than they may have anticipated. Blame it on blending— the term Congress uses to describe its plan to mix a little of the old tax structure with a little of the new in 1987.

As you recall, in the bad old days now coming to a close, taxpayers paid taxes under a graduated system of rates that ranged up to 50 percent. In the better days signaled by tax reform, there are supposed to be only two rates—15 percent and 28 percent.

Now, as a reasonable person you assume that these simple rate changes took effect when President Reagan signed the bill into law. But they didn't.

In the lawmakers' judgment, rate reduction was simply too enormous for the tax system to absorb all at once. So they opted to combine the old rates with the new for 1987.

The year-end net effect on the taxpayer? A first-year top marginal rate not of 50 percent, nor the promised 28 percent— but an in-between figure of 38.5 percent.

Before we continue, let's define two key terms:

• Effective tax rate is the overall rate at which you pay tax on all your taxable income. If you pay taxes, for example, of $5933 on $35,000 of taxable income, your effective tax rate comes to 17 percent ($5933 divided by $35,000).

• Marginal tax rate is the rate you pay on your last dollars of earnings. For example, if your taxable income is $45,000 in 1987, and you receive a $5000 bonus, your marginal rate on the bonus—if you are married filing jointly—is 35 percent, that is, the rate you pay on taxable income in the $45,000 to $50,000 range.

You also use your marginal tax rate to determine the tax benefit of a deduction. If your marginal tax rate is 35 percent, a $1000 deduction saves you $350 in tax.

Now, here are the tax rate schedules for tax years beginning in 1987:

1987 RATES AT A GLANCE

Taxable Income	Rate
Married Filing Jointly, and Surviving Spouses	
Zero to $3,000	11 percent
$3,001 to $28,000	15 percent
$28,001 to $45,000	28 percent
$45,001 to $90,000	35 percent
$90,001 and above	38.5 percent
Head of Household	
Zero to $2,500	11 percent
$2,501 to $23,000	15 percent
$23,001 to $38,000	28 percent
$38,001 to $80,000	35 percent
$80,001 and above	38.5 percent
Single	
Zero to $1,800	11 percent
$1,801 to $16,800	15 percent
$16,801 to $27,000	28 percent
$27,001 to $54,000	35 percent
$54,001 and above	38.5 percent
Married Filing Separately	
Zero to $1,500	11 percent
$1,501 to $14,000	15 percent
$14,001 to $22,500	28 percent
$22,501 to $45,000	35 percent
$45,001 and above	38.5 percent

THE NEW FLAT TAX   For some taxpayers marginal tax rates don't stop at 28 percent—even after 1987.

Take a closer look at the tax system for 1988 and beyond, and you'll see that single filers with taxable incomes exceeding $43,150 and married joint filers with $71,900 are subject to another Congressional wrinkle called a "phase-out surtax."

Instead of paying 15 percent on part of their income and 28 percent on the rest (as less well-off taxpayers do) these taxpayers get hit with an additional 5-percent tax on the upper ends of their earnings. The idea is to subject upper-income taxpayers to a flat tax of 28 percent on *all* their taxable income—not just the amount above a certain level.

Specifically, for tax years beginning after 1987 an extra 5-percent tax is assessed—in addition to the 28-percent tax—on taxable income that falls in certain ranges. These ranges, which will be adjusted for inflation for tax years beginning after 1988, are:

- Married individuals filing joint returns and surviving spouses $71,900 to $149,250
- Heads of household $61,650 to $123,790
- Single individuals $43,150 to $89,560
- Married individuals filing separate returns $35,950 to $113,300

The surtax sneakily converts what looks like a system of two brackets into a four-bracket system. Here's an example of how it works.

Say you file a joint return and your taxable income in 1988 is $75,000. The amount of your income subject to the 5-percent surtax is $3100 ($75,000 less $71,900). So this additional tax comes to $155 (5 percent times $3100).

Here's what's really happening. In effect, your entire income is being gradually subjected to a flat 28-percent rate. But the combined effect of the 28-percent rate, plus the additional 5 percent, makes a portion of your income taxable at a marginal rate of 33 percent (28 percent plus 5 percent) in 1988.

Now suppose in 1988 you and your spouse reported taxable income of $149,250. Your tax liability would be computed as follows:

- First $29,750 of taxable income at 15 percent   = $ 4,462.50
- Remaining $119,500 at 28 percent   =   33,460.00
- 5 percent of $77,350 excess over $71,900   =   3,867.50
                               $41,790.00

So you pay $41,790 total taxes in 1988.
To determine your effective tax rate, divide the total tax by

your total taxable income—$41,790 divided by $149,250. You get 28 percent.

So at $149,250 in taxable income for a married couple filing jointly, the benefits of the 15-percent tax bracket have been totally eliminated by the 5-percent surtax.

You've been hit by an overall 28-percent rate when a 33-percent tax is applied to taxable income in the $71,900 to $149,250 range.

WHERE DID ALL THE GOODIES GO?   Income-averaging. The two-earner deduction for married couples. The $100 ($200 joint return) partial dividend exclusion. Savor these Internal Revenue Code plums while you can, because soon all three will be kaput. They're gone for tax years beginning after 1986.

And here are some other goodies you lose under tax reform:

• The partial exclusion for unemployment compensation benefits for amounts you receive after 1986. Starting in 1987, expect to pay taxes on all unemployment benefits.
• The exclusion for scholarships or fellowship grants made after August 16, 1986 and received after 1986. The new law limits the exclusion to degree-seeking candidates.

Also, you may exclude from income only amounts used for tuition and books, equipment, supplies, and other required course fees.

Amounts designated for room, board, or incidental expenses are fully taxable. Also, students may now pay tax on payments made to them for teaching, research, or other services that are required as a condition of receiving the scholarship or fellowship.

WILL LESS EQUAL MORE FOR YOU?   The new rates are higher than we originally expected, but they still produce savings, right? Well, bear in mind that Congress is also lowering the boom on deductions, and that's one change that, for the most part, isn't being postponed.

Most deductions are changed as of January 1, 1987.

For lower-income taxpayers who take few deductions, the lower rates will mean a reduction in their 1987 tax bills—even with blending.

Middle- and upper-income taxpayers may not fare as well.

The extent to which they've used deductions in the past will determine if they win or lose—or just break even—under the new tax rates.

For example, wealthy taxpayers who used many tax-slashing techniques may find that the decrease in the rates is not enough to offset their loss of deductions.

Since almost everyone will give up some deductions, the big question is: How much can you give up without increasing your tax bill from 1986?

The charts below show—for three typical taxpayers—the approximate amount of deductions you could lose in 1987 and 1988 before your tax liability increases.

They take into account the changes in the tax rates, the new surtaxes and increased personal exemptions (see Chapter 3), but they ignore the effects of the alternative minimum tax, special deductions for the elderly and the blind, and the repeal of credits and income-averaging. The charts assume that you itemize deductions in 1986, 1987, and 1988.

These three scenarios should provide you with a reasonably good picture of what might happen in your own situation under reform.

Of course, the only way to know for sure is to make detailed calculations based on your own income and deductions.

So keep a scorecard as you read the later chapters.

Total deductions that can be lost
without increasing your tax bill

1986 Taxable Income*	Single, No Dependents	
	1987	1988
15,000	2,652	2,250
20,000	2,063	2,341
25,000	2,009	2,288
30,000	1,617	2,845
35,000	1,551	4,013
40,000	1,980	5,529
45,000	2,717	6,614
50,000	3,717	7,978
55,000	4,272	9,341
60,000	5,165	11,217
70,000	7,633	15,762
80,000	10,101	20,308
90,000	12,786	27,564
100,000	15,773	35,421
120,000	21,747	51,136
140,000	27,721	66,850
160,000	33,695	82,564
180,000	39,669	98,279
200,000	45,643	113,993
250,000	60,578	153,279
300,000	75,514	192,564
400,000	105,384	271,136

*Itemized deductions not reduced for ZBA (see pages 20–21).

Total deductions that can be lost
without increasing your tax bill

1986 Taxable Income*	Married, Joint Return No Dependents	
	1987	1988
15,000	1,647	947
20,000	3,147	2,447
25,000	5,319	5,207
30,000	4,933	5,415
35,000	5,058	5,540
40,000	5,951	6,433
45,000	5,803	7,326
50,000	6,123	8,976
55,000	6,551	10,761
60,000	6,980	12,547
70,000	8,854	15,307
80,000	10,854	18,034
90,000	11,939	20,882
100,000	13,627	24,519
120,000	17,588	32,473
140,000	23,043	43,837
160,000	28,497	58,837
180,000	34,170	74,137
200,000	40,144	89,851
250,000	55,079	129,137
300,000	70,014	168,423
400,000	99,884	246,994

*Itemized deductions not reduced for ZBA (see pages 20–21).

Total deductions that can be lost
without increasing your tax bill

1986 Taxable Income*	Married, Joint Return Two Dependents	
	1987	1988
15,000	3,287	2,687
20,000	4,787	4,187
25,000	6,959	6,947
30,000	6,573	7,155
35,000	6,698	7,280
40,000	7,591	8,173
45,000	7,443	9,066
50,000	7,763	10,716
55,000	8,191	12,501
60,000	8,620	14,287
70,000	10,494	17,047
80,000	12,494	19,774
90,000	13,579	22,622
100,000	15,267	26,259
120,000	19,228	34,213
140,000	24,683	43,910
160,000	30,137	56,678
180,000	35,810	71,978
200,000	41,784	87,692
250,000	56,719	126,978
300,000	71,654	166,264
400,000	101,524	244,835

*Itemized deductions not reduced for ZBA (see pages 20–21).

CHAPTER 2

IN YOUR BEST INTEREST
Congress Puts the Squeeze on Interest Deductions

CHANGES AT A GLANCE

Old Law	New Law
All home mortgage interest is fully deductible	Mortgage interest is deductible on first and second homes only
Personal interest is fully deductible	The personal interest deduction is phased out between 1987 and 1991
Investment interest deductions are limited to net investment income plus $10,000	Investment interest deductions are limited to the amount of net investment income

Under the old law, an interest expense was an interest expense. And with few exceptions, such as interest on money you borrowed to purchase tax-exempt bonds, all interest paid was deductible. It didn't matter why you borrowed the money or from whom.

But life isn't so simple anymore. Under the Tax Reform Act some interest is still deductible. Most is not. For tax years beginning after 1986, the new law zaps deductions for "personal" interest—interest you pay on automobile loans, credit cards, student loans, charge accounts, and so on.

The new law also eliminates deductions for interest paid on federal or state tax underpayments, and interest paid by an employee on property that he or she uses to perform job-related services—for instance, interest on a car loan where the employee uses the car for business. In addition, it affects imputed interest expense on personal-use loans with a below-market rate of interest.

Here's an example. Say your parents make you an unsecured $15,000 interest-free loan to help you make a down payment on a new house. Assuming de minimis rules on gift loans are not met, your parents are considered to have received an interest payment from you. Under the old law you had deductible interest expense. Under the new law you have nondeductible personal interest. Your parents have interest income in both cases.

The effect of the change in the personal interest rules: It may prod Americans into carrying less debt. Or it may encourage them to bundle their debts into those categories of loans—such as home mortgages—that still qualify for an interest deduction. As we'll see, though, this option has some limitations too.

THERE'S NO PLACE LIKE HOME   Interest on your home mortgage loan is still deductible after 1986. For most people this will be the only tax-deductible expense they have—and still the best tax shelter.

You may also write off interest on a qualifying second home, such as a vacation house. (See Chapter 6 for more information.) However, the interest paid on a refinancing may cause you to pay alternative minimum tax. (See Chapter 14.)

CLOSING A LOOPHOLE   As originally written, the new law lets you deduct interest for consumer purchases by borrowing against your home. Tax professionals made note of this loophole. And so did lawmakers. Then they closed it.

As a result you may not claim a deduction for interest paid on that portion of a mortgage loan that at the time the debt is incurred is greater than the purchase price of your property—plus the cost of any improvements you've made. However, in no event—including the exceptions noted below—may you treat a mortgage as a qualifying mortgage on a first or second home to the extent it exceeds the fair market value of the property at the time the debt is incurred.

This requirement will prevent people from borrowing against the appreciation in their homes, using the money to pay off their consumer purchases, then deducting the interest.

But the law does make a few exceptions: You may still write off interest on that part of a mortgage or equity loan that tops the purchase price and cost of improvements, if you use the excess loan proceeds to pay educational or medical expenses. If you take out a personal loan not secured by these residences—to send your daughter to college, say—the interest on that loan is not deductible.

Qualifying medical expenses are those for which you can take a medical expense deduction, except for medical insurance premiums. Medical expenses for which you are reimbursed do not qualify.

Qualifying education expenses include the tuition, fees, books, supplies, and any reasonable living expenses while attending a school or college. This includes attendance by you, your spouse, or dependents.

Let's say you decide to refinance your home, which is worth $150,000. You originally paid $80,000 for it and have made $20,000 in improvements—including adding a family room and remodeling the kitchen. The bank will let you refinance up to $120,000. But you may write off the interest on only $100,000 ($80,000 purchase price plus $20,000 of home improvements).

If you accept the bank's $120,000 offer, the interest the bank charges on $20,000 of the loan, or one-sixth—$20,000 divided by $120,000—is nondeductible personal interest expense if used for other than trade or business or investment purposes.

However, if you use $20,000 of the loan proceeds to pay educational or medical expenses, all interest on the $120,000 refinancing is tax-deductible.

For purposes of applying the limitation on home mortgages, a special provision is made for mortgages obtained on or before August 16, 1986. For these, the amount of the home cost and improvement shall not be considered to be less than the principal amount of the mortgage on August 16, 1986. This special exception helps those people who refinanced their homes while interest rates were low and obtained a mortgage greater than their cost and improvements.

BYE-BYE CREDIT BUY   Nothing in the reformed tax law says you can't use your credit card to buy a television, or that you can't take out a bank loan to finance a new set of wheels. And as mentioned earlier, if you're an employee, it doesn't even matter if you use that new set of wheels 100 percent for business. But you can no longer deduct the interest on these or any other personal-use loans from your taxable income. The change means that buying on the installment plan for most people will be more expensive than ever before.

The following chart shows the amount of personal interest you may deduct for tax years beginning after 1986.

INTEREST DEDUCTIONS AT A GLANCE

Year	Amount deductible
1987	65 percent of all personal interest
1988	40 percent of all personal interest
1989	20 percent of all personal interest
1990	10 percent of all personal interest
after 1990	none

If you have personal interest expense of $500 in 1987, your tax deduction that year is $325 (65 percent times $500). The same $500 charge in 1988 will produce a $200 tax deduction in 1988 (40 percent times $500). So the after-tax cost of borrowing gets higher as the years progress.

THEY GET YOU COMING—AND GOING   Interest you pay to the IRS, state, or local tax authorities is personal interest. So, after 1986, challenging tax assessments carries an extra cost if you lose and did not pay the assessment previously. If you have a settlement to negotiate with the IRS, you would be well advised to do so soon to avoid a possible 1986 year-end rush to settle cases. In addition to normal holiday vacations, federal employees must "use or lose" excess accumulated leave before the first pay period of 1987.

INVESTMENT INTEREST   Congress changed many of the rules relating to investment income, expenses, and interest expense. These changes look small, but their impact on some investors' tax bills won't be.

Here's a rundown of the new rules that apply to tax years beginning after 1986.

The interest you pay on investment debt—the interest, say, on your stock margin account—is still deductible, but only to the extent you have net investment income (investment income net of investment expenses other than interest). Before tax reform you added whatever net investment income you had to a $10,000 allowance to figure your limitation for investment interest deductions.

For example, you have $4000 of investment interest expense and $1000 of net investment income. In 1986 you deduct all $4000, because your limitation is equal to $11,000 ($10,000, the basic amount, plus net investment income of $1000).

Under the old law you could deduct all your investment interest expense as long as it didn't exceed your net investment income by more than $10,000. But now you're out of luck. If, in 1991, for example, you purchase investment property on credit, and have no net investment income for that year, you may deduct none of your interest payments in 1991, since there is no longer a $10,000 allowance.

Investment interest carryforward rules remain unchanged. If you run up investment interest charges that you can't deduct because they exceed your net investment income, you may carry forward the excess and treat it as a deduction in a future year. You treat it the same as investment interest actually paid in a future year.

In addition to the items included in the determination of net investment income under old law, investment income will include long-term capital gains, and income or loss from certain working oil and gas interests. However, net investment income will not include any rental (or any other passive activity) income or loss, and investment interest expense will not include interest incurred to purchase an interest in a passive activity. (However, as discussed below, during 1988 through 1990 some of the passive activity losses may be included.)

In computing investment expenses, the 2-percent of adjusted gross income (AGI, a term which means the sum of your income less certain deductions such as IRA's) floor on miscellaneous itemized deductions will be applied first to investment expenses and, therefore, possibly increase your net investment income. However, if you have miscellaneous itemized deductions other than investment expenses, such as unreimbursed employee expenses, those noninvestment expenses are considered offset first by the 2-percent-of-AGI floor.

TAKE FIVE   To soften the impact of these changes, the new law phases in the investment interest rules. In each tax year beginning during the period 1987 through 1990, the $10,000 allowance on excess investment interest will be gradually eliminated. During this period disallowed investment interest will be first computed as if the new law were fully effective, with one exception. Passive activity losses deductible under the passive loss phase-in provisions, other than the type eligible for $25,000 real-estate rental passive loss allowance, are deducted in computing net investment income.

So you compute your tentative disallowed investment interest expense based on the above. The actual disallowance during the 1987 to 1990 transition period is equal to: the applicable percentage (see chart below) on the first $10,000 ($5000 for married, filing separate returns) of the disallowed interest deduction, plus 100 percent of the disallowed investment interest above $10,000 (if any). All investment interest disallowed during the transition period is carried forward, but utilization is subject to special limitations during the transition period.

Here's the breakdown:

Year	Percentage of first $10,000 tentative disallowance
1987	35 percent of the first $10,000 disallowed
1988	60 percent of the first $10,000 disallowed
1989	80 percent of the first $10,000 disallowed
1990	90 percent of the first $10,000 disallowed
After 1990	The new law is fully effective

THE LAST WORD   Congressional tax writers have already suggested further revisions in this transitional rule so more changes are expected. One way you might avoid the investment interest limitation problem of the new law is to reorganize your personal investment debts through a mortgage on your first or second home. But remember, you may only deduct interest on a mortgage that is no more than the lesser of the cost of your home plus improvements, or its fair market value.

Another strategy to minimize the effect of the new limits on interest: Pay cash whenever possible.

CHAPTER 3

UNKINDEST CUTS OF ALL
What Those Shrinking Deductions Mean to Your Tax Bill

CHANGES AT A GLANCE

Old Law	New Law
Sales tax is fully deductible	Sales tax is not deductible
Personal exemption of $1080	1987: $1900 1988: $1950 1989: $2000
Standard deduction 1986: Married, joint return: $3670 Head of household: $2480 Single: $2480	1987: Married, joint return: $3760 Head of household: $2540 Single: $2540 1988: Married, joint return: $5000 Head of household: $4400 Single: $3000
State and local income taxes and property tax are fully deductible	The law is unchanged
Charitable contributions are deductible by itemizers and nonitemizers	Charitable contributions are deductible by itemizers only
Miscellaneous itemized deductions are fully deductible	Miscellaneous itemized deductions are subject to a 2-percent-of-AGI floor

Certain unreimbursed employee expenses are deductible as nonitemized deductions	Unreimbursed employee expenses are deductible only as miscellaneous itemized deductions

Congress calls it "base-broadening." What does it mean? Simply that more of your income will be subject to tax.

The Tax Reform Act is billed as revenue-neutral. The government must collect the same amount of taxes as it would have under the old law. The only way for Congress to accomplish this feat—at the same time it slashes tax rates—is to increase the amount of some taxpayers' income subject to taxation. The lawmakers achieve this end by taking away deductions.

The result: The full benefits of reduced tax rates are diminished by the loss of deductions.

STARTING AT ZERO   Beginning in the 1987 tax year, there will be increases in the standard deduction (previously referred to as the zero bracket amount, or ZBA).

The standard deduction is the amount all of us (except some dependents) may deduct whenever we file an income tax return. It is the threshold, or floor, for determining whether or not you can itemize, so it plays a big role in how your final tax bill looks.

Say, for example, that you're a married couple filing a joint return. In 1988, your deductions must exceed $5000—the new standard deduction for this category—before you would itemize.

The standard deduction also determines whether or not you must file a return at all. If your taxable income, after you take your personal exemption, doesn't exceed the standard deduction, you're home free.

Here's a rundown of the new standard deductions.

• Married couples filing jointly and surviving spouses. If you fall into this category, your standard deduction climbs from $3670 in 1986 to $3760 in 1987. But the biggest boost comes in 1988—to $5000.

• Heads of households. This group has the sharpest rise in the standard deduction. It goes from $2480 in 1986 to $2540 in 1987 and $4400 in 1988.

• Single people. If you're single, you have a smaller standard deduction. It rises from $2480 in 1986 to $2540 in 1987 and $3000 in 1988.

• Married couples filing separate returns. It rises from $1835 in 1986 to $1880 in 1987 and $2500 in 1988.

• Elderly and blind individuals. People who have reached age sixty-five or are blind may deduct the 1988 standard deduction for their filing category in 1987. In addition to claiming the significantly larger 1988 amount in 1987, they may increase the standard deduction in 1987 by $600 if they are married or $750 if single. If they are blind and age sixty-five or over, they add $1200 to the standard deduction in 1987 if married, $1500 if single.

When you come to the standard deduction line on your 1987 return, you may think you're getting a break. Rest assured, you're not. All that's been changed is the mechanics of taking the deduction. Under the old law, the ZBA was worked into the tax tables.

You paid zero tax on the first bracket, which was equal to the ZBA. Starting in 1987, though, the standard deduction is removed from the tax tables.

Remember, starting in 1989, the standard deduction will be adjusted upward for inflation. For example, if inflation is 3 percent, the deduction climbs 3 percent (but so does the threshold for benefiting from itemizing deductions).

YOU'RE EXEMPT The Tax Reform Act also provides a sizable increase in each taxpayer's personal exemption—the amount you subtract from your taxable income for yourself and your dependents. This is the first such increase in nearly a decade, except for annual inflationary adjustments that started in 1985.

The new law hikes the 1986 $1080-per-person figure to $1900 in 1987, $1950 in 1988, and $2000 in 1989. The 1989 amount will also be adjusted for inflation starting in 1990.

Unlike the change in the standard deduction, the increase in the personal exemption is a boon to itemizers and nonitemizers alike—with a few exceptions.

Very high-income taxpayers will see the tax benefits of their personal exemption deductions gradually phased out, much as their 15-percent tax rate is phased out at higher income levels.

The lawmakers accomplished this phase-out by a surtax that begins when the 15-percent-bracket phase-out surtax ends.

The personal exemption phase-out surtax takes effect in tax years 1988, in an amount equal to 5 percent of taxable income exceeding these levels:

• Married individuals filing joint returns and surviving spouses	$149,250
• Heads of household	$123,790
• Single individuals	$89,560
• Married individuals filing separate returns	$113,300

These levels will be adjusted for inflation in 1989—just as the 15-percent-bracket surtax ranges are adjusted for inflation. The personal exemption surtax continues as taxable income goes over the threshold, until the tax benefit of all personal exemption deductions is totally eliminated.

The amount of the personal-exemption surtax is limited by the number of exemptions you claim. For 1988, each exemption you take translates into a maximum surtax of $546. That's 28 percent (the maximum tax table rate) times $1950 (the personal exemption amount in 1988).

For 1988, you can determine when the $546 personal exemption surtax is reached by adding $10,920 for each personal exemption you claim to the surtax threshold that applies to you. (See above.)

All this is really not as complicated as it seems. For example in 1988 you, a single filer, have $100,000 of taxable income. You claim one personal exemption—yourself. Your 1988 tax liability, including surtaxes, is computed as follows:

• First $17,850 of taxable income at 15 percent	=	$2,677.50
• Remaining $82,150 at 28 percent	=	$23,002.00
• Surtax for 15 percent bracket— $46,410 (or $89,560 minus $43,150) at 5 percent	=	$2,320.50
• Surtax for personal exemption deduction— $10,440 (or $100,000 minus $89,560) at 5 percent	=	$522.00
		$28,522.00

So you pay $28,522.00 total taxes in 1988.

Since the 15-percent bracket surtax is fully phased out at taxable income of $89,560, you escaped paying that surtax on your taxable income above $89,560. Also, since your income was less than $100,480 (or $89,560 plus $10,920), you did not get slapped with the full $546-per-personal-exemption surtax.

One more point: As we've seen, Uncle Sam hits you with a 33-percent marginal tax rate if you fall in the 15-percent-bracket phase-out surtax range.

But that 5-percent surtax is averaged with the lower 15-percent bracket in reaching a 28 percent effective, or overall, rate.

When the 5-percent personal exemption phase-out surtax kicks in, the effective rate is already at 28 percent. The result: In the example above, you're paying at a 28.5-percent effective tax rate ($28,522 total tax divided by $100,000 total taxable income).

The surtax on the personal exemption deduction brings another change: the dependency exemption for children of divorced parents, formerly more valuable to the higher-paid parent, may now be more useful to the lower-earning parent. In fact, it may help only the lower-income parent.

Under the old law, the exemptions were more valuable to the higher-earning parent, since that spouse was usually in a higher tax bracket.

Another point to bear in mind: Persons who are blind or age 65 or older—though they now get a higher standard deduction—no longer may take the additional personal exemptions allowed under the old law.

ITEMIZED DEDUCTIONS—R.I.P.   Itemized deductions are subtracted from your adjusted gross income. Before tax reform, AGI equaled your gross income reduced by a handful of write-offs, including some employee business expenses, the working married-couple deduction, and your IRA contribution.

Your other deductions—the ones you subtract from your adjusted gross income—are known as below-the-line or itemized deductions. And you won't find in the Tax Reform Act some of the itemized deductions you may once have used to reduce your tax bill.

If you don't itemize, of course, you get no tax benefit from the expenses you pile up, since you take the standard deduction instead of writing off actual costs.

We might as well begin with the casualties and get the worst news out of the way first.

Most important, the new law does away with the itemized deductions for sales tax and personal interest. (See Chapter 2.) If you incur these expenses after December 31, 1986, don't expect to write them off—at least not entirely.

Since keeping track of the actual amount of sales taxes paid during the year involved a lot of recordkeeping, most people just took the amount of their sales tax deduction from an IRS table. Even if you used the table, however, you could increase the table amount for sales tax paid on a major purchase, such as a car or a boat.

For tax years beginning after 1986, you may no longer claim a sales tax write-off for taxes paid on so-called personal-use items. Also, sales taxes paid on the purchase of property, such as a depreciable business or investment asset, must be included in the property's cost for tax purposes.

You still get a full write-off for local and state income taxes, which for most people is worth a lot more than the deduction for sales taxes. Of course, if you hail from Florida or some other states that impose no state personal income tax, your deduction for taxes will consist only of property taxes, since that write-off was also saved under the Tax Reform Act.

The new law also repeals the deduction for adoption expenses for tax years beginning after 1986.

FOOTLOOSE, BUT NOT QUITE FANCY-FREE   For tax years beginning after 1986, travel expenses you run up for educational travel—where the travel itself is the educational activity—are not deductible. Also, charitable contribution deductions for travel expenses you incur while performing personal services for a charitable organization may not be deductible. (For more on both these changes, see Chapter 21.)

SWEET CHARITY   For tax years beginning after 1986, only itemizers may take a charitable contribution deduction. This rule, however, is a sin of omission—not commission—in the new tax law.

Charitable contribution deductions for nonitemizers first became effective in 1982. At that time Congress slapped a 1986 expiration date on the provision. When the lawmakers debated the new bill, they decided to let the old law stand as is. So the law expires as originally planned.

SOLDIERS OF WAR, SOLDIERS OF GOD   Under the Tax Reform Act a person who receives a parsonage or military housing allowance tax-free may still deduct otherwise qualifying home mortgage interest and real property taxes. There's other good news: The provision is retroactive. And that may translate into tax refunds for anyone who didn't take these deductions previously because he or she received a tax-free housing allowance.

BE COOPERATIVE   Under current law a tenant-shareholder in a cooperative housing corporation (co-op) is allowed a deduction for a proportional share of interest expense and real estate taxes paid by the co-op. Under pre-reform law that proportional share was, for tax purposes, determined by reference to proportional share of co-op stock owned by the tenant-stockholder. Under the new law a co-op may elect to allocate interest and/or real estate tax deductions to tenant-stockholders based on the reasonable share of the costs allocable to each unit if that is the method followed by the co-op in charging tenant-stockholders. For example, if some tenant-shareholders were to prepay their shares of the co-op's indebtedness, only those not prepaying shares would be allocated interest expense deductions for tax purposes—assuming the co-op elected this special treatment and only charged interest to those not prepaying. The election once made is revocable only with the consent of the IRS.

Additional changes in this area include extending the pass-through of the interest and real estate tax deductions to corporations, trusts, and other entities that hold stock in a co-op.

The changes applicable to co-ops are effective for tax years beginning after 1986.

ALTERED STATES   Not all itemized deductions bit the dust. Most of the survivors, however, exist in an altered state, so assumptions about what's deductible and why based on the old tax code won't do you much good.

Under tax reform, miscellaneous itemized deductions are only deductible—and therefore reduce your income taxes—to the extent they exceed 2 percent of your AGI.

While you had to exceed the zero bracket amount (ZBA—the

predecessor of the standard deduction) in the past, the increased standard deduction (see Chapter 1) and the 2-percent floor on miscellaneous itemized deductions will make it even harder for some people to itemize after 1986.

For tax years beginning after 1986, the following expenses are deductible only to the extent that, in the aggregate, they exceed 2 percent of your AGI:

* Investment advisory or management fees.
* Trust administration fees.
* Investment travel and entertainment expenses (after the new 80-percent limitation—see Chapter 21).
* Subscriptions to investment publications.
* Attorney's fees incurred in collecting income.
* Safe deposit box rental.
* Tax counsel and tax preparation fees.
* Appraisal fees for a casualty loss or for charitable contributions.
* Costs of pursuing a business that is considered a hobby under tax law (see "More Profit, More Often," below).
* Unreimbursed employee business expenses. (See "The Employee Business Expense Rules," below.)
* Any continuing education course.
* Subscriptions to professional journals.
* Union or professional dues.
* Work uniforms.
* Job-hunting expenses.
* Business use of a personal residence (meaning a home office).

The 2-percent floor does not apply to the following itemized deductions:

* Otherwise qualifying deductions for interest, taxes, casualty losses, charitable contributions, and medical costs.
* Impairment-related work expenses of handicapped employees, such as the purchase of special tools.
* Deductions for estate taxes paid on "income in respect of a decedent" (meaning estate taxes paid on income not subject to income taxes at death).
* Deductions under the "claim of right" doctrine. (These write-offs apply to situations when you receive income in one year and you return some or all of the funds in a later year, because the original payment was in error.)

- Deductions for amortizable premiums on bonds you hold.
- Expenses of short sales (in the nature of interest in a short sale, you sell borrowed property, usually stocks or securities).
- Deduction for an unrecovered investment in a terminated annuity (see Chapter 10).
- Deductible gambling losses. (These losses, however, are still limited to the amount of gambling winnings.)
- Unreimbursed employee expenses of certain actors earning less than $16,000 per year.

You may still deduct moving expenses that are due to a change in your employment. So if you accept a job in a new city and meet the IRS guidelines, you may deduct the expenses of moving to that city. However, moving expenses that were deductible "above the line" before the new law become "below-the-line" deductions under the new law. But they are not subject to the 2-percent floor after 1986.

FIRE, STORM, SHIPWRECK, AND THEFT   Deductible casualty losses are also exempt from the 2-percent floor. The limitations on these losses—in force under the old law—continue to apply under the Tax Reform Act, and reform adds one more to the list.

If your personal-use property is covered by insurance and you decide not to file a claim—for whatever reason—you may not deduct the amount of the casualty loss that your insurance policy would have reimbursed you. It doesn't even matter that you are not the primary beneficiary under the policy, as long as you could file a claim.

So if your loss is covered in whole or part by a policy, you must file a timely insurance claim, or your loss will be disallowed to the extent covered by insurance. This new provision does not apply to trade or business property or investment property—only your personal-use property.

This rule flies in the face of previous court decisions that held that failure to file a claim did not affect deductibility. Be that as it may, the provision becomes effective for losses you sustain after 1986 in tax years beginning after 1986.

THE EMPLOYEE BUSINESS EXPENSE RULES   Some unreimbursed expenses you run up as an employee may still be partially deductible—but not in the old way. For tax years beginning after 1986, they are considered miscellaneous itemized deductions and subject to the 2-percent-of-AGI floor.

These expenses include:

- Unreimbursed "away-from-home" business travel, meals, and lodging.
- Unreimbursed local business transportation.
- Unreimbursed expenses of "outside salespeople," such as manufacturers' representatives who solicit orders away from their employers' places of business.

For example, you are a full-time outside salesperson for a business machine company. Your position requires you to call on current and prospective customers in an effort to solicit sales. Since you visit your customers at their convenience, your duties include making scheduled rounds to all the businesses in your sales territory.

The expenses you incur while soliciting new business—taking customers out to dinner, for instance—are not reimbursed by your employer. So you may write them off as deductible outside-salesperson expenses, subject to the 2-percent-of-AGI floor.

The write-offs, however, are first subject to the new 80-percent limitation on meal and entertainment expenses. (See Chapter 21.)

Even if you're not an outside salesperson, you may include in your miscellaneous itemized deductions the cost of traveling between customers—in town and out of town—as long as the travel is in the interest of your employer.

But there's a difference here that is bigger than the 2-percent floor. Under the old law both itemizers and nonitemizers could deduct unreimbursed employee transportation, travel, and outside-salesperson business expenses. But by merely reclassifying these deductions as itemized—or below the line—the new law ensures that taxpayers who do not itemize will lose the write-off entirely.

MEDICAL EXPENSES—ONLY MAJOR MEDICAL NEED APPLY
Beginning in 1987 you may deduct only those medical expenses that exceed 7.5 percent of your adjusted gross income. This new rule increases the old law's limit, which allowed you to write off all medical expenses that topped 5 percent of your AGI.

On the plus side, the full costs of many home improvements

made by physically handicapped persons now qualify as medical expenses. These improvements include: ramps; railings; widening of hallways and doorways; and adjustments to cabinets and the like to make them more accessible.

The new code also contains a big break for self-employed taxpayers who pay for their own and their family's health insurance. For tax years beginning after 1986 and before 1990, these taxpayers may deduct 25 percent of the cost of this insurance "above the line"—or directly from their gross income. However, the deduction will not reduce your self-employment income when it comes time to figure self-employment tax.

The other 75 percent is lumped together with other medical expenses. So it's deductible to the extent that it and your other medical costs total more than 7.5 percent of your adjusted gross income.

To qualify for this favorable treatment, 5 percent owners must provide nondiscriminatory coverage to all their employees in all unincorporated businesses of which they own at least 5 percent.

Also, you must not be eligible to participate in the health insurance plan of an employer. And, as a self-employed taxpayer, you may not take the 25-percent deduction for health insurance premiums to the extent they exceed your adjusted earned income from the activity.

For example, you report a loss of $4000 from your unincorporated business. Your health insurance costs total $1600. Under the new law you may not write off above the line 25 percent of your medical insurance premiums, or $400, because the deduction would simply allow you to take a larger loss.

One note of caution: As mentioned above, you may not use the medical premiums you deduct from your taxable income to reduce your self-employment income when computing self-employment taxes. And remember, too, this break applies only to tax years beginning after 1986 and before 1990.

MORE PROFIT, MORE OFTEN   Uncle Sam doesn't mind if you dabble in a little business just for the fun of it. But he doesn't want to help foot the bill—hence, the so-called hobby loss limitation rule.

Under the rule, you may deduct your hobby expenses only up to the amount of your hobby income. But no more. You're not allowed to use losses from your hobby to slash your overall tax bill.

A number of activities, of course—horse breeding, farming, antique collecting, coin collecting, and boat chartering, to name a few—may not show a yearly profit. But you may in good faith be trying to make a profit. So the IRS developed two tests to determine if your business is profit-oriented or a hobby.

First, there is a subjective "facts-and-circumstances" test. Under this rule the IRS considers whether you operate your business in a businesslike way. It also examines your expertise in your chosen activity, the time and effort you devote to it, and the amount of personal pleasure you derive from it.

And second, the IRS provides an objective test. Under the old law you had to demonstrate that you'd realized a profit in two out of the most recent five consecutive taxable years. And, if you were in the horse breeding or racing business, you had to realize a profit in two of the most recent seven years. If you met these tests, the government presumed you were engaged in a legitimate business, not just a hobby.

The drafters of the new law, though, thought it too easy for taxpayers to manipulate their income and expenses to meet the objective test. Abuses could still crop up, they decided, even though the facts-and-circumstances test could override the statutory test. So they made the statutory requirements much stricter.

Now, for tax years after December 31, 1986, you must realize a profit from your business in three out of the most recent five consecutive years. The lawmakers decided to keep the former test for horse breeding and racing, though. So if the sport of kings is your passion, you still need to make a profit in only two out of seven consecutive years.

For example, Dan, a certified public accountant, owns a large sailboat that he uses four months out of the year. During the week—and on holiday weekends—he enjoys the boat with family and friends. On the remaining weekends he leases his sailboat for chartered cruises.

Dan advertises his charter service in several local newspapers and magazines and fully expects to make a profit. He first started operating his sailboat charter service in 1983. Since that time he has made a profit in two years and shown a loss in the other year. He also anticipates a loss for 1986.

Because of the change in the law, Dan will now have to realize a profit in 1987 to meet the statutory test. If he is unable to show a profit in 1987, he'll have two choices: He can demonstrate that his charter operation was not a hobby under the facts-and-circumstances test; or he can amend his previous year's tax returns to eliminate the losses that he claimed in these earlier years.

Hobbyists beware: The new law may also restrict your deductions for a hobby to an amount less than your hobby income. Here's how. Hobby deductions—other than taxes you can deduct as a personal expense, such as property taxes—are classified as miscellaneous itemized deductions and deducted below the line. As mentioned earlier, after 1986 you may claim miscellaneous deductions only to the extent that they come to more than 2 percent of your AGI.

So while you must include the full amount of your hobby earnings in taxable income, your hobby write-offs will offset this income only to the extent your combined miscellaneous itemized deductions exceed the 2-percent floor. If your combined miscellaneous itemized deductions are less than 2 percent of AGI, you get no tax deduction for your hobby expenses.

THE LAST WORD   For year-end strategies on maximizing tax benefits of continuing and expiring deductions, see Chapter 15.

CHAPTER 4

HAVEN HELP US
A Last Chance to Cash in on Long-Term Capital Gains

CHANGES AT A GLANCE

Old Law	New Law
You may exclude 60 percent of your long-term capital gains from your taxable income	You may no longer exclude 60 percent of long-term capital gains
The 60-percent exclusion resulted in a top capital-gain tax of 20 percent	Capital gains are taxed at ordinary rates, except in 1987, when the long-term capital-gain rate is capped at 28 percent

One of the best features of the old tax law was the favorable treatment accorded long-term capital gains. If you held on to an investment for more than six months, then sold it, you were taxed on only 40 percent of your profits.

The Tax Reform Act zaps this advantageous rule for tax years beginning after 1986. Beginning in 1988 long-term capital gains will be taxed at the same rates as ordinary income, such as salaries, interest, and dividends. Short-term capital gains are already taxed at the same rates as ordinary income.

For all practical purposes, after 1987 a distinction no longer exists between investments held for less than six months and those held longer.

For those presently in the top 50-percent bracket, the change means a big increase in the taxes you pay on income from long-term investments—a hike in the rate of tax of as much as 8 percent of your long-term capital gains. For those now in lower brackets, the increase can be much more.

BUY LOW, SELL HIGH   Under the old law investors excluded 60 percent of their long-term capital gains from taxation. Say, for example, that you score big in the 1986 bull market and pocket a handsome $50,000 profit when you sell your 2000 shares of Automation, Inc. Since you've held the stock for more than six months, you report a long-term gain on your tax return.

You may exclude 60 percent of this long-term gain from taxes. So you pay tax on only $20,000 (40 percent times $50,000).

How do you figure your tax liability? You add your $20,000 net capital gain to your other income. You were in the 50-percent tax bracket before the gain was added.

The result: You owe Uncle Sam $10,000 on your $50,000 net gain—that is, your net gain times 40 percent (the portion of the gain subject to taxation) times 50 percent (your bracket).

But if you pocket the same profit after 1986, when the new law is in effect, your tax rate on the gain jumps 8 percentage points. The "reformed" law no longer excludes 60 percent of your net long-term capital gain from taxation. So the entire $50,000 profit is added to your taxable income. That $50,000 is then taxed at your new tax rate—which, luckily, has gone from a top marginal rate of 50 percent to 38.5 percent in 1987 and 28 percent in 1988. And, as we'll see, the long-term capital gain tax you pay in 1987 is capped at 28 percent.

So if you recognize the $50,000 long-term capital gain in 1987 you pay $14,000 ($50,000 times 28 percent) on your profit—instead of the 1986 tax of $10,000—or $4000 more. But you will probably still be a winner under tax reform in 1987, since your maximum tax on your other income will drop 11.5 percent to 38.5 percent.

And beware: In 1988 and following years, that gain may be taxed at 33 percent, due to the 5-percent surtaxes. (See Chapter 1.) The repeal of the long-term capital-gain deduction goes for all long-term capital gains taxed after 1986. And the provision applies even though the sale took place before 1987 but is taxed after 1986, as in the case of an installment sale.

WITHIN LIMITS   As we've seen, the new 15 and 28 percent tax system won't be fully operational until 1988. So, in 1987, some people will pay taxes at rates as high as 38.5 percent, but the tax on long-term capital gains will be capped at 28 percent for 1987.

Say you and your husband report taxable income in 1987 of $200,000, with $1000 representing a long-term capital gain. A savvy investor, you report no capital losses.

Under the new law, you pay a 28-percent tax on your long-term gain—or $280—an 8-point increase. But your other income is subject in 1987 to a maximum tax rate of 38.5 percent.

RICH IS BETTER   The cap on capital gains, though, primarily benefits wealthier filers. The increase in tax on the same $1000 long-term capital gain can be much greater than 8 points for those who are presently paying tax far from the 50-percent rate.

Here's why. Assume you and your husband file a joint return for 1987 reporting taxable income of $33,000—$1000 of which is a long-term capital gain.

Under the new law you pay the top rate—28 percent—on the entire $1000 gain. Your bill adds up this way under the 1987 blended tax:

- 11 percent times $3000, or $330.
- 15 percent times $25,000 (taxable income in the $3000 to $28,000 range), or $3750.
- 28 percent times $4000 (taxable income in the $28,000 to $32,000 range), or $1120.
- Total tax equals $5200.

Your long-term capital-gain tax is: 28 percent times $1000, or $280. Your total 1987 tax is $5480.

For you and your husband, the 28-percent cap on long-term capital gains made no difference, since your highest tax bracket never got above the 28-percent rate. Nonetheless, your tax on the $1000 gain is $280, the same amount as our high-income couple in the previous example.

Much has been made of the fact that the wealthy—with big capital gains—will be hit the hardest by the increase to 28 percent of the long-term capital-gains rate. But it is actually middle-income filers in 1987 and afterward who see the biggest boost in long-term capital gains.

Had you recognized the same amounts in 1986, your marginal tax rate on the gain would have been 11 percent. For you the new law means a 17-percentage-point increase in the marginal tax rate on long-term capital gains.

WINNING BY LOSING   Under the old law you could offset in full your short-term capital losses against your short-term and long-term capital gains. But you could not subtract more than $3000 in losses from ordinary income in any one year.

Say you report a $1000 long-term capital gain and a $5000 short-term capital loss in 1986, putting you $4000 in the red. You may write off only $3000 of your $4000 loss, but you get to carry forward the remaining $1000 short-term capital loss.

But what happens if the facts are reversed, and your $5000 capital loss is long term and your $1000 gain short term? Then a whole other set of rules comes into play.

You can deduct just 50 percent of the $5000 net long-term loss in excess of the $1000 net short-term gain, subject to the same $3000 limitation. The deductible loss comes to $2000, and you used all the $4000 loss to produce the $2000 deduction.

The Tax Reform Act retains the $3000 ceiling and carryforwards of losses. But it permits you to deduct 100 percent of your losses up to $3000 a year—regardless of whether they are short or long term.

GETTING GOING WHILE THE GOING IS GOOD   The old law allowed you to postpone reporting the proceeds from the sale of securities until the settlement date, which is a few days following the day of the sale.

If the trade date and the settlement date of a stock transaction straddled a year-end, you could, if you desired, postpone recognizing the gain until the year in which the settlement date fell.

Not only did you get to choose the year you wanted to recognize your gain, you didn't have to make the decision until you filed your income tax return—normally the following April 15 (or even later if you applied for an extension). So you had at least three-and-one-half months to see how the following year was shaping up to decide in what year it would be best to recognize your gain.

The 1986 Tax Reform Act nixes this practice for stock sold

after December 31, 1986. From that date on you must report your gains from the sale of stock on the day the transaction takes place—even though the settlement date is in the next year or your broker won't write a check until days later.

The bottom line: You may use this tactic to defer income from 1986 to 1987 but not to postpone income from 1987 to 1988.

THE LAST WORD   Before you call your broker to sell your stocks in 1986, see Chapter 15 for long-term and short-term capital-gain-and-loss strategies.

CHAPTER 5

BRAVING A NEW WORLD
Real Estate Investments
Can Still Work for You

CHANGES AT A GLANCE

Old Law	New Law
Deductible losses on real estate aren't limited	Deductible losses on real estate are capped at $25,000—reduced for taxpayers with adjusted gross incomes over $100,000
Losses are deductible regardless of whether you actively participate in managing the property	Losses are not deductible within the $25,000 cap unless you actively participate in managing the property
Losses from real estate may be used to offset income from other sources	Losses in excess of $25,000 may be used only to offset gains from other passive investments
Real estate properties are depreciated over nineteen years	Residential rental properties are depreciated over 27.5 years; non-residential rental properties are depreciated over 31.5 years
Real estate investments are not subject to ''at-risk'' rules	Real estate investments are subject to ''at-risk'' rules

When Congress adopted the 1986 Tax Reform Act, it didn't turn out the lights entirely on real estate tax breaks. But in many respects the party is over.

For starters, the new law zaps attractive nineteen-year depreciation for residential rental property and commercial real estate. It eliminates the use of accelerated depreciation. And it imposes new restrictions on deductible rental-property losses.

However, the new law does provide incentives for investing in certain types of real estate. The chosen few: rehabilitation and low-income housing projects.

In this chapter we show you how Congress changed the fundamentals of real estate ownership.

TIME BANDIT   Under the old depreciation schedules you could deduct from your taxable income each year for nineteen years a portion of the cost of the investment property you purchased. And you could use the favorable accelerated depreciation method. (See Chapter 20 for more on depreciation.)

The new law stretches to 27½ years the time it takes to recoup investments in apartments and other residential rental property. Depreciation schedules for commercial real estate, such as office buildings and warehouses, run even longer—31½ years. Moreover, you must now use the less generous straight-line depreciation.

And what a difference these changes in the rules make. For example, you and another executive pool your savings and purchase a small warehouse in an industrial park. The price tag: $400,000, of which $85,000 is allocated to land.

You begin leasing the space the first of March. But the law treats your transaction as if you placed the warehouse in service in the middle of the month.

Known as the "mid-month" convention, this rule for real property comes into play the first year of ownership. It dictates that the depreciation allowed in the first year is determined by the number of months the property was actually in service.

And for the first month the tax law arbitrarily considers all real estate placed in service in the middle of the month. In this case, since you started leasing the warehouse in March, you are entitled to 9.5 months of depreciation for the year.

Using the straight-line method, your depreciation deduction in the first year comes to $7917—that is, the warehouse cost of $315,000 divided by 31½ years, with the result divided by twelve months, then multiplied by 9.5 months.

Under the old law—using accelerated depreciation—your deduction would have totaled $22,995 ($315,000 times 7.3 percent) for the first year (7.3 percent is the percentage of the purchase price you could write off the first year under the accelerated depreciation schedules)—a difference of $15,078.

One final note: Investors may also opt to depreciate real estate over forty years, instead of the usual 27½ years for residential rental property and 31½ for commercial real estate.

The advantage of this alternative method: Depreciation deductions aren't added back to your income when it comes time to figure your alternative minimum tax (AMT) liability. The alternative minimum tax is paid by those who—by taking advantage of various sections of the law—would pay little or no tax despite their high incomes.

Generally, the more heavily sheltered you are—that is, the more you take advantage of accelerated depreciation and other techniques to drive down your taxable income—the more likely you are to be in an AMT situation. (See Chapter 14 for details on the alternative minimum tax.)

ALL DELIBERATE SPEED   The old law provided two methods for depreciating residential rental property and commercial real estate—the accelerated method and the straight-line method—and it allowed investors to choose between the two.

With accelerated depreciation the annual tax deduction was "accelerated" in the first years you owned the property, so you garnered larger write-offs in those early years. With the straight-line method, write-offs remained the same from year to year.

Let's see how our warehouse transaction would fare under the two depreciation methods. You'll remember that the warehouse costs $315,000. So, using straight-line depreciation, you would write off $10,000 each year for 31½ years. The first year you may deduct only $7917 because of the mid-month convention.

Using accelerated cost recovery under the old law, you would deduct $22,995 in year one; $26,775 in year two; and $24,255 in year three. After year three the amount you could write off would continue to decrease each year until year ten. At that point the old law would require you to switch to straight-line depreciation until the warehouse was fully written off.

Generally the new law prohibits the use of the accelerated method for real property placed in service after 1986. Only the straight-line method is allowed.

BENEFITS RETAKEN   The mandatory use of the straight-line method of depreciation should not be a major impediment to commercial real estate ownership though. The reason: Many investors already use it.

Here's why: If you used the accelerated method of depreciation, Uncle Sam took back—or recaptured—many of your earlier benefits when it came time to sell your property. And the amount recaptured was considered ordinary income—that is, it was taxed at your regular tax rate. Only the gain over the amount recaptured received favorable capital-gain treatment.

Specifically for residential rental property, Uncle Sam recaptured the difference between:

• Any depreciation deductions you took under the accelerated formula; and
• Those you would have realized had you used the straight-line method.

For nonresidential real property depreciated using the accelerated method, this rule was even harsher: You recaptured all depreciation deductions.

Here's an example. You and your partner sell an apartment building you've owned for five years for $130,000. The building originally cost you $100,000.

During the time you owned the building, you took depreciation deductions using the accelerated method. The deductions you wrote off during the five years totaled $46,000. If you had used the straight-line method, your depreciation deductions would have been only $33,000.

Your gain on the sale is $76,000 ($130,000 sales price less $54,000 remaining undepreciated cost). Your depreciation recaptures amount to $13,000 ($46,000 accelerated depreciation less $33,000 straight-line depreciation). The remaining gain of $63,000 is a capital gain. So you pay taxes at regular rates on $13,000 and capital-gain rates on $63,000.

If this had been an office building instead of an apartment building, the results would change dramatically. The recapture amount would increase to $46,000 (100 percent of the depreciation). The capital gain would be reduced to $30,000.

After 1987, however, this rule will lose much of its significance. The reason: Capital gains will be subject to the same tax rates as ordinary income.

FOR RICHER, FOR POORER   Beginning in 1987 the new law limits the amount of passive losses you may deduct to the amount of income from your passive investments. (See Chapter 7 for details.) Generally rental real estate activities are considered to be passive, so they are affected by these new restrictions.

However, Congress did throw a bone to "moderate-income" taxpayers who own rental real estate—that is, those individuals with adjusted gross income (AGI) of $100,000 or less. And partial relief is provided for those with adjusted gross income up to $150,000.

The lawmakers reasoned that you might have cash-flow difficulties with investments that were genuinely designed to provide financial security, not shelter income. So if you qualify as a moderate-income taxpayer, you may deduct up to $25,000 of your net loss from passive activities against your regular income. But this exception only holds true to the extent that the loss is from the rental of either commercial or residential property. And you must actively participate in the operation. We tell you what this means a little later in the chapter.

Say you have two passive real estate investments: residential property you actively operate, and a limited partnership investment. You incur a $15,000 loss on the residential property; your share of the limited partnership's loss for the year is $10,000. The result is that your net loss from passive activities is $25,000. However, only the $15,000 loss from the residential property, which qualifies as an investment in which you actively participate, can be deducted against your regular income.

For taxpayers with adjusted gross incomes of more than $100,000—figured before you subtract rental or other passive losses—this deduction begins to phase out. And it disappears altogether for those with incomes over $150,000. For married couples filing separately, these levels are cut in half.

Here's how the phase-out works. If your adjusted gross income is less than $100,000, you may deduct as much as $25,000 in rental losses—no questions asked—in which you actively participate. If your AGI tops $100,000, you must reduce the limitation by 50 percent of the amount that your adjusted gross income exceeds $100,000.

Say your AGI before any rental or passive losses comes to $130,000. You subtract the $100,000 income ceiling from your $130,000 AGI and get $30,000. Then you multiply 50 percent times $30,000 and subtract the result—$15,000—from $25,000.

So you may write off only $10,000 under the active participation rule.

At $150,000 the amount you may write off under this rule is zero. And any losses disallowed are subject to the tough new passive-loss rule.

The IRS will phase in this rule gradually, however. In 1987 you may still deduct 65 percent of your losses from rental properties considered to be passive, 40 percent in 1988, 20 percent in 1989, and 10 percent in 1990.

After that year, though, your losses limited under these restrictions carry forward.

Another important point: You won't profit from the phase-in rules unless you own the property before passage of the new law. In addition, the expenses that you rack up in generating losses must be "ordinary and necessary" and incurred for maintaining investment property.

For example, the costs of traveling to the local lumberyard to buy materials to repair the roof of your apartment building would be ordinary and necessary. The costs of traveling to Europe to purchase the same materials—even though you can get a slightly better price—would not.

SAME TIME NEXT YEAR   Any losses you can't take because of the AGI limitation or the phase-in rules may be carried forward and deducted in future years—but only if you have enough passive income in those years. Eventually you may deduct these losses when you dispose of your real estate investment. (See Chapter 7 for more details.)

Assume you and your spouse own and manage a multifamily apartment building and file jointly. In 1987 the rental property generates a loss of $30,000. Your adjusted gross income, without the rental loss, adds up to $90,000. You do not have any passive income.

You may write off a rental loss of $28,250 for the year: the $25,000 active participation loss allowable plus $3250 (65 percent of the additional $5000 loss) allowed under the phase-in rules. You may carry forward the unused $1750 loss and treat it as a passive loss in a subsequent year.

IT PAYS TO BE ACTIVE   The new law won't allow you to write off losses up to $25,000 from rental properties unless you actively participate in their operation. This "active participation test'' is less stringent than the ''material participation test'' that applies to other passive activities. (See Chapter 7.)

The bottom line: As long as you make significant and bona fide management decisions, you meet the test. Using a rental agent will not, by itself, leave you out in the cold.

The management decisions that count, as far as Uncle Sam is concerned, include approving tenants, deciding on rental terms, and approving capital or repair expenditures.

One last wrinkle: You won't meet this requirement if your real estate is owned through a limited partnership or for any amount of time that you hold less than a 10-percent ownership interest.

What happens if you don't actively participate—or if you own less than a 10-percent interest? Your rental loss is considered ''passive,'' and you may not deduct it from your regular income. You may deduct it only from income generated by other passive investments.

RISKY BUSINESS   The old law excluded real estate investments from the government's strict ''at-risk'' rules. But not the new Tax Reform Act: It treats the holding of real estate the same as it treats other investment activities.

Under the ''at-risk'' rules you are limited to the amount of losses you may deduct. Specifically, these deductions cannot exceed the total of:

• Your cash contributions to the business;
• The adjusted basis of your property contributions to the business; and
• Any amount you borrowed for the business—but only to the extent you have personal liability or pledge other personal assets as security for the borrowing.

Significantly, the lawmakers made an exception for ''qualified nonrecourse financing''—financing secured only by the property itself. To qualify, the nonrecourse financing must be:

• Secured only by the real property;
• Considered to be actual debt (and not disguised equity, such as convertible debt); and
• Obtained from a qualified lender, which can be a bank, a savings and loan, or a related party. (If obtained from a related

party such as the seller or the promoter of the investment, it must be commercially reasonable and substantially similar to loans made to unrelated parties.)

THE LAST WORD   One final bit of good news: The new law does provide a tax credit for owners of rehabilitation and low-income residential rental properties. (See Chapter 19 for details.) Furthermore, if you have already invested in low-income housing projects, the lawmakers have provided some relief. Any losses you incur are not treated as passive. But this only applies to certain low-income housing investments made after 1983.

There is a limit. Only the losses incurred for up to seven years from the year you made the original investment qualify for this benefit. However you cannot take a low-income housing credit from the project if you are entitled to this relief.

CHAPTER 6

HOME SWEET SECOND HOME
New Rules for Writing Off Vacation Homes

CHANGES AT A GLANCE

Old Law	New Law
Mortgage interest is fully deductible	Mortgage interest is deductible only on first and second homes
Deductible losses on rented vacation homes are not limited	Deductible losses on rented vacation homes are capped at $25,000; this cap is reduced for taxpayers with adjusted gross income over $100,000 a year
Losses are deductible regardless of whether you actively participate in managing the property	Losses are not deductible within the $25,000 cap unless you actively participate in managing the property
Real estate is depreciated over nineteen years	Residential rental properties are depreciated over 27½ years

If you own, or are considering buying, a vacation home, beware. The Tax Reform Act packs some unpleasant surprises for you.

The new law shouldn't affect you much if you use your home for personal enjoyment only. As in the past, you may still deduct in full mortgage interest and property taxes on your second home. (But if you own more than two houses, you're out of luck: You may now deduct interest on only two of your homes.)

But what if you rent out your vacation hideaway? For starters, you're subject to the same strict rules that govern other types of rental property. Specifically:

• The new law extends the time required to depreciate your property.
• It sets limits on the amount of taxable losses you may claim on your personal return.

The lawmakers also kept in place some restrictions in the old law. For example, there are limits on how much you may deduct for expenses, such as maintenance and utilities, when you rent your home part of the year but also use it for a certain number of days yourself.

WHAT IS A VACATION HOME?   You may think of a vacation home as a seashore cottage or a mountainside cabin. But the law defines a vacation home in broader terms.

Any piece of property that is a "dwelling unit"—defined as containing "basic living accommodations"—may qualify. So houses, apartments, and condominiums count as vacation homes, and so may boats and house trailers.

ON YOUR OWN   The law allows you to take a loss on part of your vacation home as rental property as long as your personal use of the residence does not exceed the greater of:

• Fourteen days; or
• 10 percent of the total number of days your home is rented at "fair rental or fair value," meaning the going rate.

So, as the owner, you may always use your home for up to fourteen days each year. If it is rented at a fair value for, say, two hundred days, you may spend twenty days in the house.

And if you own two or more vacation homes, you may use each of them for the greater of fourteen days or 10 percent of the fair rental time. If you go over the time limits, Uncle Sam classifies your property as a "residence" for the year. The result: The deductions you may take are limited to the rental income from the property.

GETTING PERSONAL In Uncle Sam's view using your home "for personal purposes" is not limited to occupying your hideaway yourself. Under the rules, you've used your vacation home for personal purposes if—on any day or part of a day—the property is occupied by:

• A person with an equity interest in the property.
• A spouse or blood relative.
• A person with whom you have a barter arrangement that lets you use some other dwelling unit for a comparable period of time.
• A person to whom the vacation home is not rented for a fair rental.

The "personal-purpose" rules apply to the first three categories even if the rent you charge is a fair value.

IT'S OFF TO WORK WE GO The lawmakers recognized that you might have to spend time in your vacation home to perform repairs or maintenance work. And they further conceded that this time isn't really "vacation." So they concluded that any day you spend in the unit for the "principal purpose" of making repairs or maintaining the property will not count as a personal-use day.

AT YOUR EXPENSE Under the old law the amount you could write off in rental losses—chiefly depreciation, repair costs, utility bills, and so on—was unrestricted as long as you didn't exceed the fourteen day or 10-percent personal use test.

But now, as with any other rental property, the amount you may deduct in rental losses on your vacation home is limited. And the amount decreases as your income rises.

The details:

• If your adjusted gross income is less than $100,000, you may deduct as much as $25,000 in rental losses from your vacation home.
• If your AGI tops $100,000, you must reduce the limitation by 50 percent of the amount that your AGI exceeds $100,000.

GET ACTIVE   Under the new law—in order to deduct up to $25,000 in losses from your vacation home against your wages, dividends, and interest—you must "actively participate" in rental operations. You meet the active participation test if you:

• Have at least a 10-percent ownership stake in the vacation home; and
• Are involved in management decisions in a significant and bona fide way.

The bottom line: If you have a 10-percent stake but aren't involved in management decisions, you're subject to the passive loss limitation rules noted below.

The management decisions that count, as far as the IRS is concerned, include approving tenants, establishing rental terms, and approving expenditures. As long as you make these major decisions, the IRS doesn't care if you use a rental agent.

What happens if you don't actively participate? You are not granted the $25,000 allowance. You may deduct your rental loss only from income generated by other passive investments, such as limited partnership tax shelters. (See Chapter 5 for more information.)

Assume you live and work in Ohio. But you also own and rent out a condominium in Arizona. You use the condo part-time as a vacation home. You hire a rental agent to collect the rent and take care of maintenance and minor repairs, but you approve all leases and capital expenditures. In the eyes of Uncle Sam you meet the active participation test.

UP TO THE LIMIT   The new law has changed depreciation rules for the worse. Instead of depreciating residential rental property over nineteen years, you must now write it off over 27½ years. And you must now use the less favorable straight-line method instead of the accelerated method. (See Chapter 20 for the lowdown on depreciating such items as furniture and fixtures.)

ALLOCATE, ALLOCATE   When you use your vacation property for both personal and rental purposes, the law requires that you allocate your expenses between the two uses.

You must write off expenses allocated to rental use in the following order:

- Taxes and interest.
- Operating expenses.
- Depreciation.

Deductible operating costs include maintenance, insurance, utilities, and any other expenses, such as advertising, commissions, professional fees, repairs, and supplies that are normally deducted for profit-oriented activities.

This allocation rule limits the deductions you may take—and it applies even if you use your vacation home for personal enjoyment only one day a year.

Let's say you use your vacation home on New Year's Day only. You still must allocate all deductible expenses between the home's personal use and its rental use. In this case, one day's worth of your vacation home's total expenses will be allocated to personal use.

You allocate rental and personal expenses by multiplying your total expenses for the year by a fraction—X over Y. Here's the formula:

- The numerator, X, equals the number of days you rented your house at a fair value during the year.
- The denominator, Y, equals the total number of days the home is used during the year, minus repair and maintenance days.

Note that when expenses are allocated to both personal and rental uses, the deduction for these expenses—other than taxes and possibly interest—is limited to the amount allocated to the rental use.

And keep in mind, you still need to monitor personal days if your adjusted gross income exceeds $100,000. If you don't, you won't be able to carry forward losses from your vacation home.

VERY INTERESTING   Under the new law you may deduct interest on mortgages secured by your principal and second homes.

Generally you may not write off interest on any part of the mortgage that exceeds the original purchase price plus improvements of your property, unless you use the money for medical or educational purposes. Then you may borrow up to the fair market value. However, if you refinanced the mortgage on your home before August 17, 1986, the amount of your original purchase price plus improvements shall not be considered to be less than the principal amount of your mortgage for purposes of this rule.

The reason for this restriction: The lawmakers wanted to prevent you from making an end run around the new personal interest deduction rules. (The personal interest deduction phases out starting in 1987.) So they made sure you couldn't take out a fat mortgage on your property, use the money to finance a luxury auto, then write off the interest as mortgage interest.

What if you own more than two residences? Each tax year you may designate which home—other than your principal one—you want to have treated as your second residence. The interest on your chosen second residence will be deductible. The IRS will treat the interest on your other residences as personal interest, which is not deductible.

A residence qualifies as your second home if you meet the personal-use limitation test. That is, your personal use of the home must exceed the greater of:

- Fourteen days; or
- 10 percent of the total number of days for which the unit is rented at fair value.

However, in order to write off losses that you incur in renting out your vacation home—subject to the $25,000 allowance—you can't exceed the personal-use restrictions.

So you can either write off a rental loss from your vacation home or classify it as a second residence. But you can't do both.

If you write off a rental loss, you won't be able to deduct the mortgage interest allocated to personal use. Instead it will be treated as personal interest, subject to the new personal interest deduction rules. (See Chapter 2 for more on the new interest rules.)

THE LAST WORD   A special provision applies to a vacation home that you rent out for less than fifteen days during the year. The rule says you may not take any deductions except mortgage interest and property taxes. But the rental income you collect isn't taxable. This is one rule that can sometimes work to your advantage.

Say your vacation home is in an area that enjoys a short popular season and extraordinarily high rents—Los Angeles during the 1984 Olympics, for instance. You may rent out your house for a princely sum for less than fifteen days and enjoy the income—tax-free.

CHAPTER 7

TAKING SHELTER
Making Sense Out of the New Tax Shelter Rules

CHANGES AT A GLANCE

Old Law	New Law
There are no limits on using losses from tax shelters to offset income from other sources	Losses from tax shelters are generally used only to offset passive income

Many of us will have a lighter tax bill in the future. However, people who invested heavily in tax shelters will not fully participate in the tax-reduction bonanza. In fact, they are one of the targets of reform.

The new law slams shut the door on tax shelters—those passive investments designed to slash an individual's taxes by producing large paper losses to offset taxable income.

Here's a rundown of the changes in the shelter rules.

TIMING IS EVERYTHING   One of the most controversial provisions of the new law: Changes in the tax shelter rules are retroactive. Under the new law losses generated by tax shelters purchased before the new law was enacted are generally subject to the same harsh restrictions as shelters purchased after that date.

One exception: Investments made before the President signs the new law benefit from a phase-in period. Under this provision a prescribed percentage of the loss that would have been disallowed under the new law will still be allowed.

The result of these changes: What may have been a sound economic investment—a tax shelter that provided tax benefits in addition to projected profits—may now be a real loser.

NUMBERS GAME   The tax shelter game—developed into a high form of investment art over the years—loses its appeal under tax reform.

First, reducing the top bracket from 50 percent to 28 percent removes much of the incentive for investing in shelters.

Under the old law a person who wrote off a dollar in shelter losses could shave as much as 50 cents off his or her tax bill.

Under the new law, the top bracket for many drops to 28 percent in 1988. So, starting in 1988, this same high earner shaves only 28 cents in taxes for each dollar deducted.

Elimination of the favorable taxation of long-term capital gains hurts too. Income from the sale or disposition of the tax shelter's assets will now be subject to taxation at ordinary income tax rates.

AT A LOSS   Under the old law investors liberally used tax shelter losses to slash their taxable incomes.

Let's say you took home $200,000 from your private law practice in 1985. But your investment in a real estate limited partnership generated a $15,000 loss for you.

The old law allowed you to subtract this $15,000 loss from your earnings to reduce your taxable income to $185,000.

The new law is much tougher. It says you may deduct these losses only from your earnings from other passive investments.

What's more, it doesn't allow you to use these losses to offset income from other sources. The law defines "income from other sources" as more than just earned income. It includes interest and dividends, as well as profits from the sale of stocks and other investments—portfolio income.

One exception to the rule: The law allows you to use losses from tax shelters to offset income from other sources when you sell the investment or it ceases operation.

Another important point: The law does allow you to carry forward your losses and use them to offset income from tax shelters in future years.

Say you invested in three limited partnerships—A, B, and C.

In 1988 partnership A generates a loss of $20,000 and partnership B a loss of $5000. But partnership C posts a profit of $10,000.

Under the new law you use your losses from partnership A and B to offset your gain from partnership C to produce a total loss of $15,000.

The phase-in rules under the new law will allow you to use 40 percent of your $15,000 loss to offset income from your salary, interest, or dividends. Then you may carry forward the remaining 60-percent balance of the $15,000 loss—or $9000—to next year. The amount you carry forward is known as a "suspended loss."

You carry forward a loss of $7200 from partnership A ($20,000 divided by $25,000 times $9000) and an $1800 loss from partnership B ($5000 divided by $25,000 times $9000).

Say, in 1989, your investment in partnership A ends. The partnership's real estate investment is sold and the proceeds distributed to all partners in a final liquidation. The sale generates passive income for you of $40,000.

Because partnership A has been disposed of completely, you may use your $7200 carryover to offset the gain on the disposition. The $32,800 of remaining income may also offset the $1800 in remaining losses you carried forward from the prior year. The balance of the gain may then be used to offset any losses generated by partnership B or C or other passive investments in 1989.

'TIS BETTER TO GIVE THAN TO RECEIVE   When you give away an interest in a tax shelter to a friend or relative, you lose your right to claim suspended losses in future years. In such cases suspended losses are added to the recipient's basis in the property and aren't available for your use. Further, sales to related parties also will not trigger immediate utilization of the "suspended losses."

INTERESTED PARTIES   Here's a break for you: The new law says investments that are subject to the passive loss limits are not subject to the investment interest limits.

For the most part interest expenses are treated as they were in the past. They're used to figure your income or loss from the investment.

And it makes no difference whether the interest is "inside interest"—meaning it was incurred by the limited partnership itself—or "outside interest," which is interest on money you borrow to purchase a share of the limited partnership.

The only impact a passive activity has on calculating interest limitations: Losses allowed under the phase-in provisions reduce net investment income for the investment interest limitation. (See Chapter 2 for more information.)

NO CREDIT   The same rules that apply to losses apply to credits. You may use tax credits passed along to you from shelters only to offset the tax on the net income from these investments.

The provision would apply mostly to a tax shelter that passes along tax credits—such as energy credits, research and development credit, and investment tax credits allowed under the transitional rules—to partners.

Also, like losses, credits may be carried forward to a future tax year. However, credits are not available for offset against tax on earned income and portfolio income when you dispose of your shelter.

You can elect to increase your basis by any "suspended" credits before the disposition. This provision results in a lower gain or higher loss on disposition of the property. If this election is made, the "suspended" passive activity credit is no longer available for carryforward.

Assume you invested in a solar-energy tax shelter that created an energy tax credit of $1000 for you in 1987. The credit would be available to offset income only if the tax shelter or some other passive activity generates sufficient income that results in a regular tax of $1000 in 1987 or a future year.

NOT SO PASSIVE   Two key phrases to keep in mind:

- Trade or business.
- Material participation.

For the most part, only investments in a trade or business (including research and experimentation activity) that are classified as passive are subject to the new limits on loss deductions. For instance, any rental activity is a passive activity.

Under the new law passive investments include businesses in which you do not "materially participate." Material participation—in Uncle Sam's eyes—means you are involved in operations on a "regular, continuous, and substantial basis."

The determination of material participation is based on a facts-and-circumstances test. Some of the factors considered when determining material participation are:

• The activity is your principal business. If you spend thirty-five hours a week operating a grocery store, for example, you are materially participating in the grocery store's operations. Although no one factor outweighs any other, in practice, you will most likely pass the material participation test if a business is your principal business.

• You are present at the place where the principal operations of the activity are conducted. For example, if you invest in a horse-breeding operation that is several hundred miles away from your home, and you do not visit your horses, you will most likely not be considered a material participant. But if you raise horses on land that is part of or near your principal home, it is more likely that you will materially participate.

• You have knowledge or experience in the business. For example, an investor's cattle-breeding experience and knowledge is highly significant in determining whether participation in management is likely to meet the material participation test.

• You provide services that are integral to the activity. For example, providing legal services to a general partnership that you invested in would not be treated as material participation.

The new law requires Uncle Sam to take a look each year at all the relevant facts and circumstances—including your "regular, continuous, and substantial involvement in operations"—and judge whether you materially participate in the business.

The sole exception: limited partnerships, which are always considered passive. A limited partnership, which is almost synonymous with the term tax shelter, is a passive investment because you don't participate in management.

SPARE ME   A few shelter benefits survived the reformers. As we saw in Chapter 5, real estate made it through reform with some tax breaks in place.

Another exception to the tax shelter rules was carved out for working interests in oil and gas properties. The exception does not apply to limited partnerships or other types of deals that limit a participant's liability. The law defines a working interest as one that includes development and operation expenses for the partner.

Losses generated by these interests are not subject to the limitations on losses from passive investments. You may deduct them from your regular income. And you don't have to materially participate in operations to do so.

SLOW AND STEADY For investments (including a binding obligation to purchase) made before the Tax Reform Act was enacted—where the activity has commenced operations (or has a binding contract in effect on August 16, 1986, to acquire assets to be used in the activity)—the law provides a five-year phase-in period. Tax shelter losses and credits that will eventually be zapped completely will be allowed to offset earned or portfolio income—or tax on this income— according to the following percentages:

- 1987—65 percent.
- 1988—40 percent.
- 1989—20 percent.
- 1990—10 percent.
- 1991—zero percent.

Although the new tax shelter rules are phased in for regular tax purposes, don't expect this generosity for the alternative minimum tax. (See Chapter 14.)

Any loss that the phase-out regulations allow you for regular tax purposes must be added back to taxable income when computing the alternative minimum tax. So the benefit you receive through reduction of your regular tax may be diluted because of the alternative minimum tax.

THE LAST WORD What's left? Not much.

The tax shelter game, as we've known it, may become extinct. The only major exception: working interests in oil and gas wells, and some forms of real estate investment.

In earlier years you should have decided whether or not to invest in tax shelters based on the rate of return. But the rate of return included substantial tax benefits.

In the future you should continue to look to limited partnerships for solid economic returns. But you'll have to exclude or minimize tax benefits when you evaluate the investment. High cash returns and current income—not losses—will make these investments worthwhile.

Remember, income and losses from all passive activities are added together. The obvious strategy is to invest in activities that will generate passive income, since the new law limits the deduction of your losses from tax shelters. Such income can then offset the losses.

So new limited partnerships that produce current income may be attractive. You may use income from these investments to offset losses from previous tax shelter investments.

Another avenue you might want to explore is investing in a profitable general partnership or S corporation that is carrying on a trade or business. For the income to be considered passive, however, you must not materially participate. IRS regulations will provide further guidance on this strategy.

CHAPTER 8

FAMILY TIES
What You Should Now Know About Family Income-Shifting

CHANGES AT A GLANCE

Old Law	New Law
Unearned income is taxed at child's rates	Net unearned income is taxed at parent's rate if the child is under age fourteen
Clifford trusts are used to shift income	Benefits of Clifford trusts are eliminated

Before passage of the Tax Reform Act, a family could slash its taxes by shifting income from one member to another. A parent in a high tax bracket could, for instance, give money or property to a child. And income generated by that gift would be taxed at the child's lower rate.

Now, while you may still shift income within the family unit, Congress has made many of the tactics used to transfer assets less useful as tax-cutting devices.

Nonetheless, family tax planning is still possible. In this chapter, we'll show you how to cash in on the tax-saving opportunities that remain.

CHILD'S PLAY   Remember the day you turned fourteen? Maybe you got a new bicycle. Or maybe your Friday night curfew got extended to ten-thirty or eleven.

Today's youngsters have something else to look forward to. Under the new tax law, when a child reaches fourteen he or she becomes a bona fide tax shelter.

Under the old law a parent could transfer cash or property, valued at any amount, to a minor child or to a trust in the child's name. And income earned on those assets would be taxed at the child's lower marginal tax rate.

Under the new law you may still make the transfer, and the assets themselves are subject to the gift-tax rules. However, the tax on your child's net unearned income is now equal to the additional tax that you would pay if the net unearned income were included in your tax return. That is, it is taxed at your marginal rate until your child reaches fourteen, assuming your marginal rate is higher than your child's marginal rate.

In other words, shifting assets to a child younger than fourteen may result in little or no tax savings at all.

This outcome, of course, is exactly what Congress had in mind. Drafters of the 1986 Tax Reform Act argued that the old law provided too much incentive for parents to turn over income-producing assets to children. Uncle Sam, as a result, was losing out on valuable tax receipts.

So lawmakers—to help pay for a cut in overall tax rates—decided to restrict this opportunity for tax avoidance. They nixed income-shifting as a major tax-saving strategy for parents with young children. But they retained it as an option for parents with older youngsters.

The reason: Income from assets transferred to a child fourteen years of age or older typically goes to finance the cost of a college education.

ALL WORK AND NO PLAY   As we've seen, if your offspring is under the age of fourteen, all net unearned income is taxed at your tax rate—not your child's. This rule is for tax years beginning after the date of enactment of the new law.

Net unearned income of a child means:

• Unearned income—interest, dividends, capital gains, and so forth—in excess of $500 (the first $500 of unearned income is taxed at the child's marginal rate).

• Reduced by the greater of: $500 of the standard deduction or $500 of itemized deductions; or deductions that are directly connected with the production of the unearned income, such as investment adviser fees.

Assume your child Bob has $700 of earned income, $3000 of unearned income, and itemized deductions of $800 (net of the 2-percent floor) that are directly connected with the production of the unearned income. Bob has $200 of other deductions.

The entire amount of the deductions relating to unearned income is allocated against his unearned income, because this amount ($800) exceeds $500. Therefore, Bob has net unearned income equal to $2200 ($3000 of unearned income less $800), of which $500 is taxed at Bob's rates and $1700 is taxed at your top rate. Bob's remaining $200 of deductions are allocated against earned income, with the remaining $500 of earned income taxed at Bob's rates.

A way to avoid this new rule on net unearned income is to have children between the ages of four and fourteen invest in EE savings bonds. EE's have a ten-year maturity and generate no taxable interest income until redeemed at maturity. You can give cash, and the child can purchase the bonds. When the bonds mature, the child will be over fourteen, and thus the interest income will be taxed at the child's tax rate and not yours.

In the case of divorced parents, net unearned income is taxed at the marginal rate of the parent who has custody. But what if the parents have joint custody or file separate tax returns? In these instances the child's net unearned income is taxed at the rate of the parent in the higher marginal bracket.

Different rules apply, however, if, say, your other son, Ben, has a job. Then the money he pockets is considered earned income and is taxed at his lower marginal rate. This holds true even if he is paying taxes at your marginal rate on his net unearned income.

So there is an additional opportunity to shift income from the higher-rate parent to the lower-rate child—even when the child is younger than fourteen. But to do so, you must be a business owner.

Say you need some part-time help in your candy store and decide that Ben, now ten, is old enough to tackle the job. For two hours a day, six days a week, Ben stocks the shelves. You pay him the going rate for this type of work—$3.50 an hour.

Ben's annual earnings of $2100 ($42 a week for fifty weeks) are taxable at his 15-percent rate. He files a tax return, but he pays no taxes. Why? Under the new law a single person must earn at least $3000 in 1988 ($2540 in 1987) before he or she is subject to taxation. The old law required a single person to pay taxes when income hit $2480.

But wait. There's more good news.

You benefit too. The law allows you to deduct the $2100 you paid Ben as a business expense, which reduces your taxable income by that amount.

Just one caveat: Make sure you do not pay your children more for the job than it is worth. Uncle Sam does not look kindly on a stock boy making $25 an hour, say, particularly if the little laborer is the business owner's minor child. And, chances are, such a deduction will be disallowed on audit.

THE OLDER YOU GET—THE BETTER IT IS   The new tax law has less effect on income-shifting strategies that involve children fourteen years of age or older. In fact, whatever tactics you have been using with your older offspring still apply—with one major exception.

The new law does preclude the use of short-term trusts that allow parents to retain the principal. (These are discussed under "Trust Me," below.)

But outright gifts of assets are still effective techniques for building college funds or other savings for your kids. You should be careful though. The money now belongs to your child. And losing control of your assets—or taking a chance that little Ben will use his funds to buy a BMW rather than pay for his college education—are risks you must weigh carefully before making a substantial gift.

Under both the old and new laws each parent may give each child of any age up to $10,000 a year ($20,000 for parents electing gift-splitting) with no gift-tax consequences. Gifts, however, of more than $10,000 ($20,000 for parents electing gift-splitting) may be subject to a gift tax. Gift-splitting allows a parent to jointly give $20,000 to each recipient—your children, niece, nephew, even a family friend.

If the child is over fourteen years of age, the earnings will accumulate faster than if you kept the assets in your own name, because of the child's lower tax rate. To see how much faster earnings build, assume that you can earn 10 percent compounded daily on $10,000 and that you reinvest the pretax earnings. And assume that your tax rate is 28 percent.

At the end of five years your $10,000 will have grown to $16,453 before taxes, and you will have paid $1807 in taxes on the earnings. So you will have netted—after tax—$4646.

Suppose, on the other hand, you had given the $10,000 to Ben's older sister, Barb, who is fifteen. Her tax rate is 15 percent. Barb's $10,000 would have also grown to $16,453 before taxes in five years. But she would have paid just $968 in taxes on the earnings. So her after-tax return totals $5485.

The bottom line: Any income-producing asset is worth more over time in Barb's portfolio than it is in yours because of her lower tax rate. Of course, you still must ask whether the benefit of a greater return—in our example, $839 over five years—is worth losing control over your funds.

DOUBLE-DIPPING   Before the Tax Reform Act, dependent children—no matter what their ages—actually counted for two personal exemptions.

Parents could claim the child on their tax return, and the child could claim himself or herself as well. The result: The parents received an exemption, and so did the child.

The double-dipping added up to substantial savings.

Here's an example. You are a taxpayer in the 50-percent marginal bracket. You subtract from your taxable income $1080 for each of your three sons—or $3240. The deduction saves you $1620 in taxes.

At the same time, each of your sons files his own tax return reporting $8800 in income from summer jobs and trust funds. Each also subtracts $1080 from taxable income. The deduction saves each child $162 in taxes (a marginal tax rate of 15 percent times $1080).

But the new law eliminates this tax advantage. Parents may still claim a personal exemption for a dependent child. The child, however, may not claim the exemption if the parents can.

A ROSE BY ANY OTHER NAME   Under the old law the standard deduction (better known as the zero bracket amount)— $2480 in 1986—couldn't be used to lower the amount of unearned income that was subject to tax.

Under the new law, though, a child may take the standard deduction against $500 of unearned income or against earned income—that is, income from wages or salary.

Caveat: The standard deduction is limited to the greater of $500 or earned income—up to $3000 in 1988 ($2540 in 1987).

For example, if the child has $800 of earned income and $900 of unearned income, the child's standard deduction is $800, of which $500 is allocated against unearned income and $300 is allocated against earned income. The child has net unearned income of $400. Since net unearned income is less than $500, the child's net unearned income is taxed at the child's rates. The remaining $500 of earned income also is taxed at the child's rates.

To compare the old law and the new, let's look at how Barb would fare under each. Assume that in addition to the $1500 she had in unearned income (from your $10,000 gift last year), she also earned $4000 working in the family candy store. So Barb's total adjusted gross income would be $5500.

Under the old law Barb could claim one personal exemption worth $1080. Her taxable income was thus reduced to $4420 ($5500 minus $1080). The standard deduction or zero bracket amount—$2480—was built into the tax rates and tax tables. So she paid no tax on that amount, and her tax liability came to just $221.

Under the new law Barb cannot claim a personal exemption. Her taxable income is now $2500 ($4000 in earned income plus unearned income of $1500 minus the 1988 standard deduction of $3000).

She pays a tax rate of 15 percent on her earned income and on $500 of her net unearned income; $500 of her net unearned income is offset by the standard deduction. So that leaves the balance of her net unearned income, or $500, subject to tax at your marginal bracket.

Her total tax bill comes to $440—the sum of the tax ($225) on her earned income ($4000 less the $2500 standard deduction) at the 15-percent rate; the tax ($75) on $500 of net unearned income at the 15-percent rate; and the tax ($140) on $500 of net unearned income at your marginal rate of 28 percent.

Oddly enough, a lot more dependent children will actually be taking the standard deduction for tax year 1987 and beyond because of another change the new law makes: It requires all dependent children with gross income in excess of the standard deduction (greater of $500 or the amount of earned income), or with unearned income of more than $500, to file a return.

Before, a person had to have investment income of $1080 or

gross income of $3560 before he or she had to file. The new requirement applies even if you owe no tax.

One last note: For tax returns filed on or after January 1, 1988 (and these include 1987 returns filed in 1988), you'll need a Social Security number for all dependents over the age of four. So if your child is over the age of four and does not have a Social Security card, get him or her one soon.

TRUST ME   Short-term trusts have long been a common technique for shifting income from a high-bracket to a low-bracket taxpayer. The most popular was the Clifford trust, named for George Clifford, the defendant in the Supreme Court case that legitimized its use.

With a Clifford trust, the grantor—the individual creating the trust—got back the cash or assets contributed to the trust after its term had expired. But for the life of the trust, depending on its terms, the earnings from these assets were taxed either to the beneficiary or to the trust. In either case the tax rates were substantially lower than the grantor's.

By law, Clifford trusts had to last for more than ten years or for the life of the beneficiary. They were useful in financing children's college educations. And they could also be used to provide support for an aging or ailing relative with little income of his or her own.

But the new law repeals the use of short-term grantor trusts, such as Clifford trusts, as income-shifting devices. From now on income and deductions generated by these trusts will be included directly in the grantor's taxable income.

The law doesn't say that you can't create a short-term trust for newborn Nancy's Harvard tuition. It just eliminates the tax benefits of doing so. You'll pay taxes on the earnings of the assets in Nancy's trust just as if you had retained them in your own portfolio.

You should also consider other sources of funds to assist the financing of your children's college education. These other sources would include home equity loans and loans from your 401(k) plan. (See Chapter 14 for possible alternative minimum tax ramifications.)

Tax law changes apply not only to Clifford trusts, but also to spousal-remainder trusts, which have become increasingly popular in recent years. People used these devices to transfer assets from one marriage partner to another. The idea was to cut estate taxes by reducing the value of the transferor spouse's estate subject to taxation. Many people, however, set up this type of trust because its life was shorter than a Clifford trust—usually around five years instead of ten years.

One piece of good news, however. The law does contain a grandfather clause. The new rules apply only to transfers in trusts made after March 1, 1986. So, transfers to Clifford and spousal-remainder trusts before that time are not affected.

Keep in mind: Even though the new law wipes out the tax benefits of these trusts, setting up a trust may still have advantages over making outright gifts. With a trust, you can direct how the funds will be used as well as assist your child in managing the assets.

In the course of revising this basic rule on trusts, Congress quashed several other trust-related tax planning opportunities.

Here's a rundown of the new rules.

Taxable Year

Under the old law, your trust could file its tax return based on the calendar year or it could choose an entirely different fiscal year. By opting for a different year, a simple trust—that is, a trust that distributes all its income annually—would defer reporting income to the beneficiary.

If, for instance, you created a simple trust for Aunt Mary that distributes all its income annually in February 1984, you could designate January 31, 1985, as the end of the trust's taxable year.

Aunt Mary pays her taxes on a calendar-year schedule. So she didn't have to report the trust income she received for the year that ended January 31, 1985, until she filed her 1985 tax return in 1986.

The new law says all trusts, other than charitable ones, must adopt a taxable year ending December 31. This change effectively ends the big benefits of tax deferral through year-end staggering.

Caveat: Because of the change, trusts with a year-end other than a calendar year-end will—beginning after December 31, 1986—have to file two returns in 1987. The first covers their previous taxable year ending in 1987. The second return picks up where the first return leaves off: that is, it covers the short period between the end of the first return and December 31, 1987.

Obviously this new rule will cause the income of affected

trusts to bunch up in 1987, accelerating the payment of tax on this income, possibly at a higher marginal tax rate. To alleviate this inadvertent penalty, Congress is allowing trusts to spread the income from this short taxable year over a four-year period, 1987 through 1990.

Multiple Trusts

Until now taxpayers could lower their tax bite by creating not one but several trusts. A small trust would be taxed at a lower tax rate than a large trust.

Why? The tax on each trust's income began at the lowest marginal rate and went up through the tax brackets as the income increased.

Let's say you created a trust that generated income of $100,000. Under the 1986 tables your tax liability was $40,881. The effective tax rate on that single trust was 41 percent.

On the other hand, had you created two trusts, each of which generated income of $50,000, the tax liability of each—according to the tax tables—would have been $16,527. Your total tax bill for the two trusts—$33,054—would be $7827 less than for the single trust. The effective tax rate on the $100,000 income, by splitting the trusts in half, would have been cut to just 33 percent.

Alas, the new law effectively eliminates multiple trusts as a tax-saving device. It taxes the first $5000 in income at 15 percent and the excess at 28 percent.

That's not so bad, you say, compared to the old top rates of 50 percent. But when the trust's taxable income reaches $13,000, the new law begins to phase out the benefit of the initial 15-percent bracket. And this benefit is entirely phased out when taxable income reaches $26,000.

In other words, at taxable income of $26,000 and above, all of a trust's taxable income is taxed at the 28-percent rate. The marginal and effective rates, under the new law, are the same when taxable income exceeds $26,000.

Quarterly Estimates

The law now requires trusts to make estimated tax payments quarterly, just as individuals who are self-employed or do not have enough tax withheld from their wages have always had to do.

This change has no effect on a trust's tax liability, but it may create headaches for trust administrators. If they underestimate the trust's taxable income, the trust may have to pay a nondeductible underpayment penalty when it files its return.

THE LAST WORD   Remember, even under the new tax law, you can still give your child, a friend, or relative as much as $10,000 during a calendar year without getting hit with a gift tax.

If your spouse agrees, the two of you may combine your bequests, raising the maximum tax-free gift to $20,000. There are some sound estate reasons for considering gifts.

For example, gift-giving within the $10,000 (or $20,000) limit per year saves the transfer taxes that would otherwise be payable on the amount of the gift when the rest of your estate is shifted to your heirs.

CHAPTER 9

ALL THAT GLITTERS . . .
IRA's—Less Gold for Your Golden Years?

CHANGES AT A GLANCE

Old Law	New Law
A working taxpayer may deduct IRA contributions up to $2000 or 100 percent of earnings, whichever is less	A working taxpayer not covered by another retirement plan may deduct IRA contributions
	A working taxpayer covered by another retirement plan may deduct IRA contributions if adjusted gross income is less than $25,000 a year ($40,000 for married couples filing jointly)
	A working taxpayer covered by another retirement plan may not make deductible IRA contributions if AGI tops $35,000 a year ($50,000 for joint filers)

Retirement: A chance, at last, to put your feet up on the porch instead of a desk—and to crack open that nest egg you've set aside.

Except that the new tax law makes setting aside that nest egg a good deal more difficult and somewhat more expensive.

After 1986 most taxpayers will enjoy less flexibility in choosing among retirement plans. And they won't be able to salt away as much tax-deferred income as in the past.

While Congress wants to ensure that everyone who wants—and can afford—a retirement plan has one, the lawmakers saw no need for high earners to make deductible contributions to Individual Retirement Accounts (IRA's) if they were already covered by company retirement plans. Legislators also wanted to make sure that people used tax-deferred plans for retirement—not just as savings accounts or shelters for income.

So with the new law Congress has limited your ability to deduct the contributions you make to retirement plans from your current taxable income. And it has expanded the penalties for early withdrawal from these plans. The crackdown applies to almost every kind of plan—from IRA's to union pension plans.

We cover the new rules governing retirement plans in this and the next chapter. We begin with IRA's, however, since nowhere else is the change in the law more dramatic.

LESS BANG FOR YOUR BUCK   Before 1981 the only people who could set up IRA's and deduct their contributions were those not covered by employer-sponsored retirement plans.

Then, in 1981, Congress voted to allow every employed person to put away money in an IRA and subtract that contribution from his or her taxable income. One other requirement though: The individual must not have turned seventy and one-half years old by the close of the tax year. By loosening the eligibility requirements for IRA's, Congress hoped to increase the national savings rate.

The IRA provision in the 1981 law allowed individuals to place the lesser of 100 percent of their earned income or $2000 per year into special accounts. You didn't have to pay taxes on either your contributions to the IRA or the earnings that accumulated—interest, dividends, and so on—until you began withdrawing your funds; in most cases, after you reached age fifty-nine and one-half.

So IRA's were a good deal, especially if you were also part of, say, your employer's qualified tax-favored pension plan.

BACK TO THE FUTURE   Too much of a good deal, in the lawmakers' view. So in its new law, Congress designates 1986 as the last year many taxpayers may make deductible IRA contributions.

The Tax Reform Act of 1986 still allows people who are

not covered by company-sponsored retirement plans to deduct their IRA contributions. But it places new restrictions on deductions claimed by high earners who participate in company-sponsored plans.

The law won't allow you to deduct your IRA contributions if you or your spouse participates in a company retirement plan and your adjusted gross income (AGI) exceeds a certain ceiling. The cap: $50,000 a year—figured before you subtract your IRA contributions—for married couples filing jointly, and $35,000 a year for single taxpayers.

If your AGI adds up to less than $25,000 a year—$40,000 for married couples filing jointly—you may make deductible IRA contributions regardless of whether you, or your spouse, are covered by a company-sponsored retirement plan.

You're entitled to a partial deduction for your IRA contribution if you're single and your annual AGI falls between $25,000 and $35,000. The same holds true for married couples with AGI between $40,000 and $50,000. For married couples—filing separate returns—the AGI spread is zero to $10,000. The IRA deduction limit is reduced proportionately as AGI increases within the phase-out range. The limitation on the IRA deduction is then rounded down to the next lowest $10—if the limit is not a multiple of $10.

Congress provides a $200 floor on the IRA deduction limit for individuals whose AGI is within—not above—the phase-out range. For example, a single individual with AGI of $34,750 would have a $200 limit on his or her IRA deduction—even though the phase-out would have otherwise provided a limit on the IRA deduction of $50.

If you may deduct only a portion of your IRA contributions—due to the AGI phase-out provision—you may still make nondeductible IRA contributions, as long as the total of the two—deductible and nondeductible contributions—does not exceed the $2000-a-year limitation. And the earnings on both accounts accumulate tax-free until withdrawn.

Let's say you earn $25,000 in 1987, and your spouse makes $10,000. Neither of you participates in a company pension plan. Under the new law each of you may make a tax-deductible contribution of up to $2000 to an IRA—for a total of $4000.

Even if you made $50,000 and your spouse earned $20,000, you may still make tax-deductible contributions of up to $2000 each.

The reason is clear: The new law says that people who are not active participants in another retirement plan may make deductible contributions—just as they did under the old law—regardless of how much they earn. For a married couple filing jointly, neither spouse may be an active participant.

Here's another example. You earn $15,000 and participate in your company's retirement plan. Your spouse also earns $15,000 but is not covered by a pension plan. The new law allows you to each make tax-deductible contributions of up to $2000 to an IRA.

The reason: The phase-out starts at $40,000 for joint filers. So even though you are covered by your employer's retirement plan, your combined AGI is only $30,000.

But alter the facts slightly and the scenario changes entirely. Say you earn $25,000 and your spouse makes $20,000. Because your AGI adds up to $45,000, the law won't allow you to make deductible contributions of up to $2000 each. But it will allow you to subtract a portion of your IRA contributions from your gross income.

Here's how you calculate the amount you may deduct. Subtract your AGI—in this case, $45,000—from the contribution ceiling—$50,000. Then divide the result—$5000—by $10,000. This percentage—50 percent—is the portion of your $2000 IRA contribution you may deduct on your return.

So, you could each make a $1000 deductible IRA contribution. In addition, you could each make a nondeductible contribution of $1000.

The results would be the same if both of you were active participants, since the phase-out for married filers kicks in if either spouse is considered an active participant.

GET ACTIVE   Uncle Sam defines company-sponsored retirement plans as:

• Qualified pension, profit-sharing, or stock bonus plans, including 401(k) plans.
• Qualified annuity plans.
• Simplified employee pension plans (SEP's).
• Retirement plans for state or local government employees.
• Certain union pension trusts (Section 501(c)(18) plans).
• Tax-sheltered annuities for employees of nonprofit organizations.

An unfunded deferred compensation plan of a state or local government or nonprofit organization is not considered a company-sponsored plan. So if you participate in such a plan, you are not considered an active participant and are not subject to the phase-out rules.

Furthermore, the definition of an "active participant" is very broad. You don't have to collect benefits from a plan to be active in it. Nor do you need to be vested, nor entitled to receive full benefits.

All that's required to classify you as an active participant—in the case of a pension plan—is that you meet the eligibility standards of the plan at any time during the tax year. You don't even have to actually participate in the plan.

With a profit-sharing plan, you are considered an active participant once an addition is made to your account—by your employer, for instance.

In the case of a 401(k) plan, you are considered an eligible participant if your company lets you defer part of your salary, and you choose to do so.

These conditions may prove particularly troublesome for some people who change jobs. For others it may provide an opportunity for tax savings.

Suppose you accept a new position with XYZ Corp. in December 1986. You will make $60,000 a year. You leave your old job at QPA Corp.—and QPA's pension plan, which has a fiscal year ending January 31, 1987.

Even if you are ineligible to participate in your new employer's pension plan during calendar year 1987, you may not make a deductible contribution to an IRA for that year. The reason: You are still considered covered by your former pension plan in 1987, and your AGI is too high.

Uncle Sam determines active participation by looking at when a company-sponsored plan year ends. So if you change jobs, you could also find yourself with a tax year when no eligible plan year ends. And, in this case, you could pocket a tax-deductible write-off for your IRA contribution.

In the above example you could make a deductible IRA contribution in 1988 if you meet one of two conditions:

• You won't be eligible for the new employer's pension plan until 1989.
• The employer's plan year for which you become eligible in 1988 operates on a tax year that ends in 1989.

Don't misunderstand: Nothing in the new law says you can't establish an IRA—up to $2000 for individuals or $2250 for an individual and nonworking spouse—as long as your IRA is deposited by the deadline for filing that year's tax return. And the earnings on those IRA deposits will still accumulate tax-free until you withdraw them. You just can't deduct those contributions from income—and neither can your nonworking spouse—if you're considered an active participant in another qualified plan.

On the other hand the new law also says that you won't have to pay taxes on the amount of those nondeductible contributions when you do withdraw them. (The accumulated earnings, however, will be taxable upon withdrawal, just as before.)

Let's say you earn $75,000 in 1987 and participate in your employer's retirement plan. You make a $2000 contribution to an IRA at your local bank. The contribution isn't deductible on your return, but the interest the IRA earns accumulates tax-free until the money is withdrawn.

In 1993, at the age of sixty-two, you retire. You withdraw the money from your IRA, which has grown to $3200. You pay tax on the $1200 of interest. The remaining $2000 is not subject to taxation, since the contribution was not deducted by you in the year it was made.

What happens if you withdraw only $2000 from your IRA? The law requires you to take out a portion of the accumulated earnings at the same time you withdraw your nondeductible contributions.

If you take out $2000, the withdrawal would not be treated as coming entirely from your nondeductible contribution. Rather, 62.5 percent ($2000 contribution divided by $3200 IRA accumulated balance)—or $1250—of the withdrawal is a tax-free return of your nondeductible contribution. And the remaining 37.5 percent ($1200 earnings divided by $3200)—or $750—is taxable income.

You still have until April 15, 1987, to make your 1986 IRA contributions. Remember, if you're covered by an employer retirement plan, 1986 is your last chance to make a deductible contribution—unless your AGI in later years falls below the phase-out threshold. So be sure to designate the deposit as being for 1986.

UP TO THE LIMIT Another warning: If you think making additional contributions to your IRA before the new law takes effect sounds smart, think again. There is still a 6-percent penalty on excess IRA contributions—that is, amounts you contribute over $2000 for an individual or $2250 for an individual and nonworking spouse.

If you've contributed too much to your IRA, you may avoid the penalty by asking the institution where you've deposited the money to refund the excess—plus any earnings on that amount—to you. You're home free as long as the refund is made by the due date of that year's tax return. Any excess contribution and earnings returned would be taxable in that year.

So excess deposits to your 1986 IRA—and any earnings that accumulate—must be returned to you by April 15, 1987, the due date of your 1986 return.

Here's another point to keep in mind. Obviously the new law will result in the mixing of deductible and nondeductible contributions in many individual retirement accounts. As we've seen, deductible contributions—and the earnings that accumulate—are subject to taxation upon withdrawal. Nondeductible deposits are not—but the earnings attributed to these contributions are taxed.

So, at distribution time you'd like to pull out the nondeductible contributions first. But Congress says no. When you withdraw funds from your IRA—if you have made both deductible and nondeductible contributions—you are taking a portion from both types. Therefore, some is returned tax-free and the remainder is taxable. To figure the tax-free portion, you divide your total nondeductible contributions by your total balance in all your IRA's. Then you multiply that percentage by the total amount withdrawn.

Assume you made nondeductible contributions in prior years totaling $3000. The balance in all of your IRA's totals $15,000. You take a withdrawal of $2500. The amount of the distribution that is a tax-free return of your nondeductible contributions is $500—$3000 divided by $15,000—or 20 percent of $2500. The remaining 80 percent—or $2000—is taxable.

IFS, ANDS, OR BUTS   The basic criterion for establishing a spousal IRA remains the same: You may create an IRA for your nonworking spouse, as well as for yourself, as long as you file a joint tax return. And your spouse must not have turned seventy and one-half by the end of the year.

The total contribution to both IRA's, however, may not total more than $2250 or 100 percent of the working spouse's wages or salary for the year, whichever is less. Just as under the earlier law, you may divide your contributions between the two accounts—yours and your nonworking spouse's—any way you choose, as long as neither spouse is allotted more than $2000.

The new law does, however, treat the nonworking spouse's IRA contribution the same way it treats the working spouse's. So if you are covered by your employer's retirement plan, you may not write off a contribution to a spousal IRA, unless your AGI is less than the phase-out threshold.

But there's good news too.

A major problem under the old law disappears under the new. Previously if the nonworking spouse had just one dollar of compensation from employment during the year—even jury duty that paid $25, for instance—the couple's total IRA contributions were limited to $2000 plus the amount of the "nonworking" spouse's compensation.

In the case of the jury duty example, that rule meant that the IRA limit for the nonworking spouse was $25. So the couple could put no more than $2025 into their IRA's.

Beginning with the 1986 tax year, however, either spouse, whatever his or her income, may choose to be treated as having no compensation in order to qualify for a spousal IRA. If one of you takes this option, you could contribute up to $2250 to your IRA's—and split this amount any way you choose between the two accounts, provided that no more than $2000 is allocated to either spouse.

NEITHER A BORROWER NOR A LENDER BE   In the days before tax reform the interest you paid on personal loans was tax-deductible. So you could write off the interest you paid on money you borrowed to make your annual IRA contributions.

Some banks cashed in on this provision. They loaned people money to contribute to an IRA so that they would keep that money on deposit.

Since tax reform, however, it makes considerably less sense to borrow to make your IRA contribution, because the interest you pay on those loans may not be deductible at all.

The new law begins to phase out the deductibility of all personal interest expense (except qualified mortgage interest) beginning in 1987. (See Chapter 2.)

EARLY BIRD   IRA funds have always been available to their depositors, penalty-free, at the age of fifty-nine and one-half—or sooner in cases of death or disability.

Like the old law, though, the new law mandates that early withdrawal of deductible contributions for any reason will cost you a 10-percent penalty. (Deductible funds, you will recall, are those attributable to IRA contributions that were subtracted from your taxable income when you made them, plus all the earnings that have accumulated on those amounts over the years.)

If your early distribution consists of nondeductible IRA contributions, no penalty will apply. The distribution of the earnings attributable to these nondeductible IRA contributions is, however, subject to the 10-percent penalty.

Beginning in 1987, though, Congress gives hale-and-hearty IRA-holders a new, penalty-free opportunity to begin IRA distributions before they reach age fifty-nine and one-half, die, or become disabled. This rule applies to both deductible and nondeductible contributions.

But there's a catch: The distributions must be made in the form of an annuity or periodic payments made to you over your lifetime.

These payments must be based on your life or life expectancy or the joint lives or life expectancies of you and your beneficiary. And they must be of substantially equal amounts and made at least annually.

Say, for example, that you contributed to an IRA each year for the last four years. On January 1, 1987, your account balance has grown to $10,000.

In 1987 you opt to withdraw the funds. Since you are only forty-five years old, you may not take the money out without forking over the 10-percent, premature-withdrawal penalty.

Here's where the new law provides you with a break: You simply instruct your IRA trustee to pay out the funds to you in regular periodic payments based on how long you're expected to live.

REPORT TO THE IRS   Under the new law you must furnish information to the IRS with your tax return for the year that you make nondeductible contributions or receive a distribution from any IRA. The IRS wants to know the amount of your nondeductible contribution for the current year, the amount of any distribution received in the current year, the excess (if any)

of your total aggregate nondeductible contributions for all preceding years over prior distributions (not included in income),
and the balance of all IRA's you have as of the close of the year.

Why does the IRS want this information? To keep track of the
amount of nondeductible contributions you have made and how
much remains available for withdrawal—tax-free.

THE LAST WORD   Here's another new provision. Under
the old law you couldn't invest your IRA money in collectibles,
such as stamps, gold and silver coins, rugs, and antiques. Under
the new law, this restriction is loosened. After 1986 you may
invest your IRA money in gold and silver coins issued by the
U.S. Government.

CHAPTER 10

THE EASY LIFE
Other Retirement Planning Options Lose Their Luster

CHANGES AT A GLANCE

Old Law	New Law
Annual additions to 401(k) plans may not top $30,000 or 25 percent of your earnings, whichever is less	Annual deferrals to 401(k) plans are capped at $7000
Uncle Sam imposes a 10-percent penalty on early withdrawals from IRA's	Uncle Sam imposes a 10-percent penalty on early withdrawals from all qualified retirement plans, not just IRA's
Taxpayers may apply favorable ten-year-averaging rules to withdrawals from retirement plans	Favorable ten-year-averaging is replaced by five-year-averaging

Just as it tightened the rules governing IRA's, Congress has scaled back the benefits of participating in employer-sponsored retirement plans.

Before we go any further, though, let's clear up any confusion about the differences among IRA's, company pension plans, and 401(k) plans.

Despite the new, tighter laws, you may still be able to use some combination of the three to feather your retirement nest egg.

Generally IRA's are retirement savings programs that you

create yourself. You—not your employer—contribute to the account. The law allows you to sock away the lesser of $2000 or 100 percent of compensation each year—$2250 if you and your nonworking spouse file jointly. And you may still deduct your IRA contribution on your tax return—as long as you're not covered by an employer-sponsored retirement plan or your AGI is below a certain level. (See Chapter 9 for the details on IRA's.)

Employer-sponsored pension plans are created by the company you work for, and for the most part the company—not you—makes periodic contributions on your behalf. As with an IRA, you pay no tax on these contributions or on any earnings that accumulate until you begin to collect the benefits, usually at retirement. Most employer-sponsored pension plans fall into one of two categories—defined-contribution plans and defined-benefit plans.

With a defined-contribution plan, a predetermined amount—say, 10 to 15 percent of your salary—is contributed to the plan for you each year. The amount you receive upon retirement is based solely on the total amount deposited on your behalf, plus any earnings that accumulate.

With a defined-benefit plan, the amount your employer contributes may vary. But you receive a set amount each year upon retirement—hence the term defined benefit.

Then there are 401(k) plans—a type of qualified cash or deferred arrangement (CODA)—created and administered by your employer. But they may or may not involve employer contributions. These plans allow employees to voluntarily stash a portion of their wages or salary into a retirement nest egg. As with an IRA, the money you put away and any earnings that accumulate are not taxable until you withdraw them—again, usually at retirement.

TO DEFER OR NOT TO DEFER   Now let's look more closely at the increasingly popular 401(k) plans. What they all have in common is this: They are funded, for the most part, by employees' elective deferrals of part of their wages.

But employers may contribute to 401(k) plans too. For example, your employer may agree to contribute or "match" 25 percent of every dollar you ante up. So if you contribute $100 per month, your employer would provide $25.

Under the old law the ceiling on annual additions—that is, employee deferrals and employer's additions—to 401(k) plans came to $30,000 or 25 percent of your nondeferred salary, whichever was less. Much too generous, concluded the legislators.

So the new law sets a much lower limit. Starting in 1987 you may defer only $7000 annually. This amount is indexed for inflation using the Consumer Price Index, beginning in 1988.

If you make additional elective deferrals under other plans—such as Simplified Employee Pensions (SEP's) or union pension fund plans—501(c)(18)—your total annual contributions to all these plans may not exceed $7000.

And watch out, lawmakers put teeth into the $7000 limit: If, for whatever reason, your total deferral to all plans exceeds $7000 in any single year, you must report the excess as taxable income in that year. And you'll have to pay taxes on the amount.

But you must also take a couple of additional steps. By March 1 of the following year you must notify the administrators of your plans that you have made an excess deferral, and you must allocate the excess among them.

The plan administrators then have until April 15 of the year following your excess deferral to return both the amount of your excess deferral (or their share of it, if you allocated the excess over two or more plans) and the earnings that have accumulated.

You must also declare those earnings as taxable income for the year during which you made the excess deferral.

There is no additional penalty. However, should the plan administrators fail to return your excess contribution—plus related earnings—by April 15 of the following year the amount remains in the 401(k) plans.

And even though you included the excess deferral in income for the year of the deferral, you'll be taxed again on the excess and its earnings when you withdraw the money at retirement. In short, you end up paying a double tax. You would owe income taxes for the year of the deferral on the excess deferral. And when you finally began drawing money out of the accounts at retirement, the entire excess deferral would be taxed again.

The new law does provide one break: It imposes no additional penalties for the withdrawals of the excess 401(k) deferrals.

Of course, these provisions of the new law are worse in theory than in practice. Unless you are among those rare individuals who participate in several plans administered by several employers in the course of a single year, your plan administrator will know if your deferral is exceeding the allowable limit and will see that you reduce it.

SOME GOOD NEWS   The $7000 limitation applies only to an employee's elective deferrals—not the employer's matching funds. So your contributions—plus your employer's—may total, annually, the lesser of $30,000 or 25 percent of earnings.

Remember too: Even though you can't defer more than $7000 in 1987, you still may have time to boost your 401(k) deferrals for the remainder of 1986—up to the limit the plan permits, or the lesser of $30,000 or 25 percent of your nondeferred salary.

ON YOUR OWN   Under both the old and new laws self-employed taxpayers may set up, in addition to an IRA, a retirement plan known as a Keogh. The Keogh may be either a defined-benefit or defined-contribution plan.

As we've seen, a defined-contribution plan lets you contribute a set amount—say, 5 to 10 percent of your earnings—to the plan a year. You may contribute as much as the lesser of $30,000 or 25 percent of your nondeferred earnings.

With the more complicated defined-benefit plan, you contribute an amount that is necessary to fund an eventual payout based on actuarial tables for your life expectancy. The annual benefit can't exceed the lesser of $90,000 or 100 percent of your average earnings for your three consecutive years of highest earnings.

You may also work for a company and still be eligible for a Keogh. If you have any self-employment earnings—from director's fees, say, or moonlighting as a consultant—you may establish a Keogh plan for this income.

The new law keeps intact most of the rules on Keoghs. One major change: If you have a defined-benefit plan, you can't receive full benefits until age sixty-five. The old law mandated a minimum age of sixty-two.

TAKING MONEY OUT   So far we've been talking about the changes the new tax law has made in the ways you can put money into retirement plans. The law's effect, for the most part, is to reduce the tax-deductible contributions you may make to the retirement plans for which you are eligible.

But the Tax Reform Act of 1986 also affects the tax consequences of withdrawing money from your various retirement funds. The details follow.

TAKING YOUR LUMPS   How should you take your retirement fund distribution? In a single lump sum? Or spread out
over time?

The obvious disadvantage to taking your accumulated savings
out of a retirement plan in a single lump sum: You may incur a
big tax liability in the year you do so. The old tax law allowed
you to mitigate that liability somewhat—except in the case of
IRA's—by using ten-year-averaging.

Under the old law you could use ten-year-averaging only once
after reaching age fifty-nine and one-half. But until then you
could use it as frequently as you liked—as long as you met the
other requirements. Among them: You died, became disabled, or
terminated your employment.

Here's how ten-year-averaging worked: You figured what you
owed Uncle Sam by first computing a tentative tax on one-tenth
of the lump-sum distribution in the year that you took it. Then
you multiplied that figure by 10.

The top tax rate on one-tenth of the distribution was usually
much lower than the top rate on the full distribution. And the
total tax using averaging was usually smaller.

For example, Sam, age sixty, retires in 1986 and elects to
have the benefits from his employer's pension plan distributed to
him in a lump-sum payment of $100,000.

Sam and his wife, Evelyn, had other taxable income in 1986
of $60,000. If Sam did not choose ten-year-averaging, he would
pay $45,517 in taxes on the $100,000 distribution.

He calculates the tax by first computing the tax on total
income of $160,000 ($60,000 other income plus $100,000 distri-
bution). The tax comes to $60,082.

Next, he calculates the tax on income other than the $100,000
distribution. The tax on $60,000 taxable income comes to $14,565.

The difference between the two represents the tax on the
$100,000 distribution—$60,082 less $14,565, or $45,517. The
$100,000 is taxed at an effective rate of more than 45 percent
($45,517 divided by $100,000).

However, if Sam had decided to use ten-year-averaging, he
would pay taxes of only $14,470 on the $100,000 distribution.
Here's how Sam would calculate the tax:

• He adds 10 percent of the distribution to a single taxpayer's
zero bracket amount ($10,000 plus $2480 equals $12,480).

• He calculates the tax on this amount using the tax rate schedule for single taxpayers (tax on $12,480 equals $1447).
• Now he multiplies this amount by 10 ($1447 times 10 equals $14,470).

Using ten-year-averaging, Sam's effective tax rate comes to less than 15 percent ($14,470 divided by $100,000), a saving of more than $31,000.

You make your tax calculation the same way under the new law—but with a difference. You replace ten years with five.

Why this change? The lawmakers decided that there was less need for averaging under the new two-tier rate structure.

Another important change: You may use five-year averaging only once. And that one time must come after you've reached age fifty-nine and one-half. Anyone younger who receives a lump-sum distribution—upon changing jobs, for instance—now has just two alternatives. He or she may either roll the distribution over into another retirement plan or accept the full tax impact of the distribution in the year it occurs. And in the latter case, the amount may also be subject to a premature distribution penalty, which we'll get to shortly.

These changes take effect for lump-sum distributions that occur after 1986. But the law does provide a transition rule.

If you were at least age fifty on January 1, 1986, you have a choice. You may use the new law's five-year-averaging—based on the tax rates in effect for the year of distribution—or the old law's ten-year-averaging, based on 1986 tax rates.

To decide which of these alternatives works out the best, just perform both calculations using the appropriate tax rates and the amount of your lump-sum settlement.

For instance, assume Sam received his distribution in 1988. The tax on a $100,000 distribution, using ten-year-averaging and 1986 tax rates, totals $14,470. Using five-year-averaging and 1988 rates, the tax totals $16,400. So Sam should select ten-year-averaging to pocket a saving of $1930 ($16,400 minus $14,470).

Be careful though. If you use the transition averaging rules before you reach age fifty-nine and one-half, you can't use the averaging provisions ever again.

BYE-BYE CAPITAL-GAIN BREAKS   Previously, if you participated in a retirement plan before 1974, you could treat part of the lump-sum distribution from your plan as a long-term capital gain. How much you could treat as a capital gain depended on the ratio of pre-1974 participation years to your total years in the plan.

Let's say you joined a retirement plan in 1964 and received a lump-sum payment in 1984. You could treat 50 percent of the payment (ten years of pre-1974 participation divided by twenty years of total participation) as a long-term capital gain.

The new law repeals this favorable long-term capital-gain treatment for any distribution you receive after 1986—just as it eliminates the tax advantages on all long-term capital gains realized on any investment sold after 1986. (See Chapter 4.)

But the lawmakers do give you a moderate break. They've enacted a transition rule for lump-sum retirement plan distributions received after 1986 and before 1992.

It works like this: First, figure the amount of the lump-sum distribution that would have qualified for long-term capital-gain treatment under the old law.

Then, to calculate how much of that amount will still qualify for capital-gain treatment under the transition rule, consult the following table:

- 1987—100 percent.
- 1988—95 percent.
- 1989—75 percent.
- 1990—50 percent.
- 1991—25 percent.

And an exception to the transition rule should help many taxpayers. Anyone who reached age fifty by January 1, 1986, may still treat all long-term capital gain determined under the old law as long-term capital gain under the new law.

This special rule applies regardless of when you receive the distribution. So you may collect it after 1991—the end of the six-year phase-out for everyone else.

People over fifty get another benefit: The current top capital-gain rate of 20 percent will apply to the capital-gain component of distributions they receive after 1986. All other taxpayers will pay the same rate on capital gains as they pay on ordinary income.

If you're not fifty by January 1, 1986, you only win under the new law if you also have capital losses. Since you may deduct only $3000 of losses that exceed your capital gains—the capital-gain component of the lump-sum distribution can soak up capital losses that you could not otherwise deduct in the current year. (See Chapter 4.)

But whatever gain remains after you net out your losses will, under the new law, be taxed at the same 15-, 28-, or 33-percent rates as ordinary income.

Suppose you began participating in a company retirement plan in 1964 and receive a $100,000 lump-sum distribution in 1989. Your pre-1974 years represent 40 percent of your total years—so $40,000 of the distribution represents long-term capital gain. But you must reduce the $40,000 capital gain by the transitional rule percentage—or 75 percent. So you may treat only $30,000 of your $100,000 lump-sum distribution as a long-term capital gain. But its real value is to allow you to soak up excess capital losses.

Unless you can soak up losses, the full $100,000 distribution is subject to taxes at the ordinary rates. The only exception: If you take your lump-sum distribution in 1987. In that year there is still preferential treatment for capital gains. The top regular rate is 38.5 percent, while the maximum capital-gain rate is 28 percent.

SPREADING OUT THE REWARDS   Instead of taking all the funds out of your employer-sponsored retirement plan in a single lump sum, you may decide to receive your benefits in the form of an annuity—annual payments whose size depends upon your life expectancy or the joint life expectancies of you and your beneficiary. (The IRS uses its Standard Annuity Tables to determine life expectancy.)

Under the old law the taxation of annuities was generous. If the total payments you received during the first three years were more than the nondeductible contributions you made to the plan, you wouldn't have to pay tax on the payments until they exceeded the amount of your contributions.

Assume you contributed $26,000 to your employer-sponsored retirement plan. You retire in 1985 and begin receiving monthly benefits of $2000. At this rate you'll recover your contributions in thirteen months ($26,000 divided by $2000).

Since the recovery period is less than three years, your first $26,000 is considered a return of your contributions. And it is tax-free. But from the fourteenth month on, your monthly payments of $2000 are fully taxable.

The new law repeals this three-year rule. For annuities beginning after July 1, 1986, every payment—starting with the first—will be part taxable and part nontaxable. The part that is nontaxable consists of that portion made up of your nondeductible contributions and is referred to as the "exclusion ratio."

So if you're counting on an annuity, check with your plan administrator to see how the new law will affect the taxation of your payments.

If you're lucky enough to live beyond your actuarial life expectancy, you will have recovered, tax-free, the entire amount of your contributions to your retirement plan. Congratulations! But get ready for a tax hike.

The new law dictates that all annuity payments received after you pass that statistical milestone will be fully taxable. So after you have fully recovered your contributions, you are no longer eligible to exclude a portion of the benefit payments from income. This change takes effect for taxpayers whose annuity starting date is after December 31, 1986.

Take some consolation, though, from knowing that should you die before reaching your full life expectancy, your heirs may take a deduction in your final tax return for the amount of your unrecovered contribution.

The rules that govern how preannuity-date withdrawals are taxed have also been tightened. Under the old law distributions you took before the annuity starting date—that is, before retirement—were treated as if they first came from your contributions, so they were tax-free. Only after these distributions were used up were amounts treated as if they were from taxable amounts—such as the earnings that accumulate. Under the new law annuity distributions received before the annuity starting date are part taxable and part nontaxable.

Take heart though. There is a transitional rule. Under it, some taxpayers may still pull out their contributions first and not pay taxes on them. To qualify for this special treatment you must participate in a plan that—as of May 5, 1986—permitted the withdrawal of employee contributions before the annuity starting date.

If you qualify, you may treat withdrawals you take after December 31, 1986, and before the annuity starting date as pre-1987 employee contributions. And they're tax-free. After you've recovered these contributions, your subsequent distributions are taxed under the new rules.

Congress did provide some relief for participants of defined-contribution plans. The employee's contributions—and any related earnings—may be treated as a separate contract for purpose of the exclusion ratio calculation. So if you withdraw contributions from such a plan, the distribution will not be attributable to your employer's contributions. The exclusion ratio will be high—that is, more returned tax-free, rather than taxable.

EARLY BIRD SPECIALS Sometimes the temptation, or the need, to tap into your retirement fund before you retire becomes too great. You just can't wait.

If that's the case for you, there are still a couple of ways to crack your nest egg before you actually reach retirement age. But the new law tightens the rules substantially.

Under the old law if you borrowed money from your retirement plan, the loan was treated as a distribution. So it was subject to tax and perhaps premature withdrawal penalties—unless it did not exceed the lesser of (1) $50,000 or (2) $10,000 or half your accrued benefits, whichever was greater.

Another condition: You had to repay your loan within five years.

There was an exception to this five-year rule: You could pay back your loan "within a reasonable period" if you used the loan to acquire or improve either your personal residence or any family member's personal residence.

Now the rules have changed for all loans made, or modified, after 1986. New or extended loans, when combined with the current outstanding balance of all other loans you've made from your plan, may not exceed an amount equal to $50,000, reduced by the excess of (1) the highest outstanding loan balance during the one-year period preceding the date of the new or extended loan above (2) the outstanding balance of loans on the date the loan is made.

For example, suppose you have outstanding loans totaling $40,000 on January 1, 1988. On August 1, 1988, you want to borrow additional money. Your loan balance for outstanding loans is $25,000. You could take out only $10,000 ($50,000 less $25,000, minus $40,000 less $25,000) in new loans in August—even if you pay off the $40,000 balance by August 1.

The effect of this provision: You may no longer "roll over" loans" or pay off a loan and reborrow the same amount in excess of $25,000.

The $50,000 limit, reduced by $25,000 for outstanding loans, leaves $25,000 available for new loans for the next year. So you could continue to roll over indefinitely a loan balance of not more than $25,000.

The new law also makes two changes to the so-called principal-residence exception: First, you may no longer use the greater-than-five-year repayment schedule for loans to improve a principal residence or purchase a second residence—only to purchase a principal one. And children, grandchildren, parents, or siblings no longer qualify as family—only you, the participant, qualify.

Moreover, the new law requires that you amortize your loan in equal payments made at least quarterly over the term of the loan. So if you have a $10,000 loan repayable in five years, you must pay back principal of $500 a quarter for five years.

And there's more. Under the old law the interest on loans you took from your retirement plan was deductible. But under the new law the deduction for interest on such loans is subject to the general limits on interest. And no deduction is allowed for interest on new loans secured by elective deferrals under 401(k) plans and tax-sheltered annuities. Loans to key employees don't qualify either.

Another change: Under the old law, employees frequently received distributions from employer-sponsored retirement plans, penalty-free, when they left the job.

In fact, the old law didn't even contain a penalty for early withdrawals because, presumably, most plans didn't allow early withdrawal—except when you changed employers.

Starting in 1987, though, you'll have to pay a 10-percent penalty on early distributions from all qualified retirement plans. Previously this 10-percent penalty applied only to early distributions from IRA's.

You have to pay the penalty on distributions you take when you leave your job before age fifty-nine and one-half. But the penalty does not apply to distributions made after death or disability. So it makes even more sense to roll over any separation-from-service distributions into an IRA or other qualified plan.

The law does provide an exception for lump-sum distributions made before March 15, 1987: If you take the distribution because you leave your job—and you choose to be taxed on the amount in 1986—you don't have to pay the penalty.

The lawmakers wrote other exceptions to this penalty into the law. There is no penalty if:

• You use the distribution to pay for deductible medical expenses.

• You receive the benefits in the form of an annuity spread over your life or the joint lives of you and your beneficiary. Payments must be substantially equal and made at least annually.

• You retire after reaching age fifty-five but before age fifty-nine and one-half No penalty applies if you meet your plan's requirements for early retirement.

• You receive distributions from an Employee Stock Ownership Plan (ESOP) before January 1, 1990.

WHERE IT ALL BEGINS   The new law also modifies the rules that dictate when you must begin taking distributions from a retirement plan.

In the past all employees—other than those who own 5 percent or more of the company—had to start receiving benefits from their company-sponsored qualified plan no later than the date they left the company or at age seventy and one-half, whichever was later.

The payments had to start by April 1 of the calendar year following the calendar year you left the company or reached age seventy and one-half.

For those who owned 5 percent or more of the company, benefits had to begin no later than April 1 following the year in which they reached age seventy and one-half—even if they were still employed by the company.

The new law imposes a uniform standard on qualified retirement plans, IRA's, and tax-sheltered annuities. No matter what the plan, the starting date you must begin taking benefits can be no later than April 1 of the year following the year you reach the age of seventy and one-half.

In the past you had to pay a whopping 50-percent-nondeductible tax on amounts from your IRA that you took later than the mandatory distribution date.

Under the new rules you pay the 50-percent-nondeductible tax on the excess of required distributions over your actual distributions. (And the penalty goes for all retirement plans—not just IRA's.)

These new rules are effective for years beginning after 1988. There's an exception for employees—other than 5-percent owners—who reach age seventy and one-half by January 1, 1988. These taxpayers may defer the distributions until they actually retire.

ON WITH THE NEW Congress didn't spend all its time reducing retirement options. It also added a couple of goodies. Here's a rundown.

With a Simplified Employee Pension (SEP) plan, an employer—rather than maintaining its own pension plan—makes contributions to the IRA's of its employees. And the employer may deduct its contributions.

The employee must include the employer's contribution in his or her gross income. But the employee may also take a deduction in the same amount. So the two offset one another.

Under the old law the maximum deduction an employee could take was the lesser of $30,000 or 15 percent of compensation. And even if your employer contributed to a SEP for you, you could still take a deduction for your own IRA contribution up to the $2000 limit.

Let's say in 1986 you make $30,000. Your employer contributes $3500 to your IRA, which is part of a SEP. You contribute $2000 of your own money to the IRA. You include the $3500 in your gross income for 1986, but you're entitled to write off $5500 ($3500 employer contribution plus $2000 for your own contribution).

Under the new law many employees may—for years starting in 1987—make elective deferrals to the SEP. But these deferrals are subject to the $7000 cap.

The new law also changes the treatment of amounts contributed to a SEP on your behalf by your employer. These amounts—plus your elective deferrals—are excluded from gross income, rather than deductible under current law.

In the case of union pension plans—called Section 501(c)(18) plans—Congress decided to allow employees to make deductible contributions for years starting in 1987. However, these contributions are subject to the same limitations that apply to SEP's and Section 401(k) plans: Namely, no more than $7000—or 25 percent of compensation—may be contributed by any one person during any one year to any single plan or combination of plans.

CHAPTER 11

TALKING TOUGH
Advice on the New Incentive Stock Option Rules

CHANGES AT A GLANCE

Old Law	New Law
Options are exercised in the order issued	Options are exercised in any order
An employer may not grant options to acquire stock valued at more than $100,000 to any one person during any one year	An employer may not grant an employee more than $100,000 in stock options that first become exercisable in any one year
Stock options qualify for favorable capital-gain treatment	The 60-percent deduction of long-term capital gains is eliminated

Nothing boosts employee productivity like owning a piece of the pie. And companies know it. That's why so many of them grant incentive stock options to employees.

With incentive stock options (ISO's), employees receive the right to purchase a specified number of shares of company stock at a specified price during a specified period.

Here's an example to illustrate how ISO's work. On January 1, your company grants you the option to buy 1000 shares of its stock at the current market price of $10 a share. The only catch: Your company requires you to purchase the shares within ten years, or you lose your option.

A year later, when your company's stock jumps to $12 a share, you exercise your option. You purchase 1000 shares at your option price of $10 a share. So you pay $10,000 for stock that's now worth $12,000.

At the time your company granted you the option, you paid no tax, because in the eyes of Uncle Sam you hadn't profited—at least not yet. You also pay no tax when you exercise your option, even though, in this case, you post an immediate paper profit of $2000—that is, the difference between the $10,000 you paid for the stock by exercising your option and the current market value of $12,000.

But you *are* subject to federal taxation a year later, when the stock zooms to $20 a share and you decide to sell out. You pay income tax on the difference between the selling price of the stock—$20 a share, or $20,000—and the amount you paid under the option—$10 a share, or $10,000.

Your $10,000 profit is taxed at favorable long-term capital-gain rates, because you held the stock for the required period of time—that is, at least two years after the option was granted, and for one year after the option was exercised. If you'd sold out early, the gain would be taxed as ordinary income—a costly provision.

LET THE GOOD TIMES ROLL   ISO's won—and lost— with tax reform.

For starters the new law zaps the favorable capital-gain rules. You may no longer exclude 60 percent of your long-term capital gains from taxation. As a result, gains from ISO's will be taxed at the same rates as salaries, bonuses, and other types of ordinary income.

An exception for 1987: The new law caps capital-gain taxes at 28 percent. So your income from capital gains won't be subject to the higher blended rates.

You'll pay 28 percent on your gains from ISO's—even if you're in the top 1987 bracket of 38.5 percent. (See Chapter 1 for details.)

THE $100,000 QUESTION   Congress adopted two other provisions affecting ISO's—both favorable.

Under the old law companies couldn't grant options to acquire stock valued at more than $100,000 to any one individual during any one year. What's more, the option price could not be less than the fair market value of the stock on the date the option was granted.

Companies determined the value of options by multiplying the number of shares granted times the price quoted in the option. For example, an option that allows an employee to purchase 5000 shares of company stock at $10 a share is valued at $50,000.

Under the new law employers determine the value of options the same way. But companies may grant stock options in any amount they choose—$100,000, $500,000, or even $1 million or more.

But here's the catch: No more than $100,000 of these options may—and here's the key phrase—"become first exercisable in any one year." So a company may grant you more than $100,000 in options in a single year, as long as the options become exercisable at a rate of no more than $100,000 per year.

TIME IS MONEY   Under the old law employees had to exercise options in the order they were granted—a rule that could produce headaches. Here's why: Sometimes an employee holds several options granted at different times and calling for shares to be purchased at different prices.

Say you hold an option to purchase 1000 shares at $20 a share, another to buy 1000 at $15 a share, and still another to purchase 1000 at $10 each. You received the $20-per-share option in 1983, the $15-per-share option in 1984, and the $10-per-share option in 1985.

The old law required you to exercise first the option you held the longest—in this case, the one at $20 a share. You couldn't exercise the one with the lowest option or purchase price if an older option remained unexercised. It didn't even matter if the oldest option was "under water," meaning it listed a purchase price that was higher than the market value.

The new law gives people in such situations a break. It says that you may exercise options issued after 1986 in any order you choose. So you may now exercise the post-1986 option that carries the lowest price tag—even if you hold options granted before 1987. But options issued before 1987 must still be exercised in the order they were granted.

Continuing with our earlier example: In addition to the pre-1987 options, assume your employer granted you an option in 1987 to purchase 1000 shares of stock for $12 per share. You may exercise the 1987 option first—even though older options remain unexercised.

However, the pre-1987 options—those from 1983 to 1985—must be exercised in order. That is, the 1983 option must be exercised before the 1984 option, and so on.

THE ALTERNATIVE MINIMUM TAX BITE   Under old law you generated a preference item—for alternative minimum tax purposes—when you exercised your ISO's. The amount: the difference between the fair market value at such time and the option price.

The same rule applies under the new law. Except that the creation of the minimum tax credit may provide relief, starting in 1987, from the alternative minimum tax (AMT). (See Chapter 14.)

In addition, starting in 1987 your basis in the ISO's, for alternative minimum tax purposes, is increased by the amount of the preference. So when you sell the stock you acquired by exercising your ISO's, your gain on the sale would be less for AMT purposes—because of your increased basis. For regular tax purposes your basis is not adjusted.

So if you have a choice of exercising your ISO's in 1986 or 1987, be sure to consider the following aspects. If you are subject to AMT in both 1986 and 1987, it may be better to defer exercising your ISO's until 1987—because of the basis adjustment and the availability of the minimum tax credit, both starting in 1987.

However, if you are not subject to AMT in 1986—but suspect that you may be in 1987—it may be beneficial to exercise the options in 1986. But be sure that the ISO preference does not push you into an AMT situation for 1986.

Another benefit of exercising in 1986 as opposed to 1987 is that your minimum holding period—that is, two years after grant and one year after exercise—will start earlier. If you exercise in 1986, you may be eligible for long-term capital-gain treatment as early as 1987—provided the two-year rule was met. And in 1987 your maximum long-term capital-gain rate is 28 percent. In 1988 your maximum rate may be as high as 33 percent.

THE LAST WORD   The new law retains some favorable tax treatment of incentive stock options—that is, you pay no regular tax on the option until you actually sell the stock. So you may still exercise your options, hold the stock, watch it appreciate—and not pay tax until you sell out. But beware: You may fall into the AMT trap when you exercise the options.

CHAPTER 12

CREDIT WHERE CREDIT IS DUE
Cashing In on Remaining Tax Credits

CHANGES AT A GLANCE

Old Law	New Law
Taxpayers receive a credit of 50 percent of their political contributions (a maximum credit of $50 for single filers, $100 for joint filers)	The political contributions credit is eliminated
Low-income working parents receive earned-income credit of up to $550	Maximum earned-income credit rises to $800
The earned-income credit is phased out between $6500 and $11,000 of adjusted gross income	1987: The credit phases out between $6500 and $14,500 of AGI 1988: The credit phases out between $9000 and $17,000 of AGI
The child-care credit is available for up to two children when head of household or both parents work	The child-care credit is retained

Fact: Tax credits are better than deductions.

A $100 tax deduction will reduce the amount of your income subject to tax, but how much money you save depends entirely on your marginal tax bracket. A $100 tax credit, on the other hand, is worth exactly that—$100—because it is subtracted directly from your tax bill.

But, alas, tax credits, like deductions, have been dramatically scaled back—or eliminated—by the 1986 Tax Reform Act. Congress sacrificed the economic incentives these credits supplied in order to help pay for the new lower rates.

DISCREDITING CREDITS   Under both the old and new laws credits are a mixed bag. Some are useful to individual taxpayers, while others apply exclusively to businesses.

In this chapter we assess the effect of the tax act on credits available to individuals and tell you how to make the most of the credits that remain.

You'll also want to read Chapter 19 for the lowdown on how the Tax Reform Act affects business tax credits. Read that chapter as well to find out about personal tax credits that relate to partnerships and S corporations.

PURELY PERSONAL   Of the tax credits that apply exclusively to personal tax returns, some have been abolished by the new law, others modified, and a few left alone.

Here's a look at the winners and losers.

LOSER: Political Contributions.

The old law allowed you to claim a credit on your personal return for half of your political contributions—but only up to a point. The law capped the political-contribution tax credit at $50 on an individual return, $100 on a joint return.

So if you donated, say, $50 to your neighbor's campaign for the state legislature, you qualified for a $25 tax credit. If you contributed $100, you earned a $50 credit. But if you kicked in $500, you still only qualified for a $50 credit.

The new law zaps this credit entirely beginning in 1987. So act fast. Capture the credit by making your 1987 political contributions in 1986.

WINNER: Earned-Income Credit.

When Congress adopted the Tax Reform Act, it not only preserved the earned-income credit, it voted to give those affected by it a substantial benefit.

In 1987 the credit jumps from 11 percent to 14 percent of the first $5714 (formerly $5000) of "earned income"—wages, salaries, and self-employment income. As a result, the maximum amount of the credit increases to $800 from $550. In addition the base amount of earned income ($5714 in 1987) will be adjusted each year to keep up with inflation.

The earned-income credit was designed to allow low-income parents with children to keep more of the money they make. To qualify for it a wage earner must maintain a household that is the primary residence of the worker and child, and the child must qualify as a dependent.

Specifically you must provide more than half of the child's support. Also, the child must earn less than the personal exemption amount—$1900 in 1987—unless he or she is under age nineteen or a full-time student.

Beginning in 1987 the maximum earned-income credit is $800. But as income exceeds $6500—$9000 in 1988—the credit is phased out so that no credit is available once income tops $14,500—$17,000 in 1988.

The phase-out works like this: The credit is reduced by an amount equal to 10 percent of your adjusted gross income—or earned income, if greater—in excess of $6500 ($9000 starting in 1988). The phase-out starting point of $6500 ($9000) will also be adjusted annually for inflation.

Say you are the mother of one child and your 1987 AGI adds up to $8000, of which $7000 is earned income. Your earned-income credit is limited to $650: $800 (14 percent times the first $5714 of earned income) minus $150 (10 percent times the $1500 excess over $6500).

Another plus: If your taxable income for the year is so low that you pay no income tax at all, the earned-income tax credit is a real blessing. Uncle Sam will send you a check for the full amount of the credit even if your tax liability is zero. Employers now must notify you if your wages qualify for the credit. This will reduce the possibility of you forgetting to claim the credit if you have it coming to you. Also, if you already know that you'll qualify for the credit, you can arrange with your employer to receive it in advance through your paycheck. Get a copy of Form W-5 and check with your employer.

WINNER: Child- or Dependent-Care Credit.

This credit remains intact under the new law.

Designed primarily to help working parents defray the cost of child care, the credit is also helpful to working people with adult dependents, such as elderly parents. For the most part, though, the credit may be taken by married couples only if both spouses are employed outside the home.

To qualify for the credit you must meet a host of requirements. For starters you must bear financial responsibility for maintaining your household, and you must spend money for the care of any of the following dependents while you're on the job:

- Youngsters under age fifteen who are dependents.
- Dependents who are physically or mentally incapable of caring for themselves—a person with Down's Syndrome or Alzheimer's Disease, for example.
- Spouses who are physically or mentally incapable of caring for themselves, because of, say, an illness or accident.

The IRS defines a dependent as either a relative or an unrelated person who is a U.S. citizen and a member of your household for the entire year. For you to qualify for the credit, your dependent must earn less than the amount of the personal exemption—$1080 in 1986—and you must provide more than half of his or her support.

The child- or dependent-care credit ranges from a low of 20 percent to a high of 30 percent of expenses paid during the year. The percentage is based on your adjusted gross income: If your AGI is $10,000 or less, the 30-percent credit applies; if it tops $28,000, the 20-percent credit applies.

What if your taxable income falls between $10,000 and $28,000? The 30-percent credit is reduced by one percent for each $2000 of AGI in excess of $10,000. For instance, a person with AGI of $14,000 would qualify for a 28-percent credit.

The credit applies only to "employment-related" expenses of up to $2400 for one dependent and $4800 for two or more dependents—so the maximum credit is $1440 (30 percent times $4800). The IRS defines employment-related expenses as the cost of people to care for your dependent or provide household services—cleaning, cooking, and so on.

If you've already topped the expense limit of $2400 for one dependent or $4800 for two or more dependents, wait until 1987 to give your baby-sitter or housekeeper a raise.

Caveat: If your dependent-care expenses exceed your earnings, watch out. Uncle Sam says the credit may be applied only to expenses that are equal to or less than your earned income.

Say you earn $2000 working part-time and your AGI is $10,000.

You pay someone $2400 to care for your child while you're on the job.

Under the law you may claim only $2000 of child-care expenses. And your credit totals $600 (30 percent times $2000), not $720 (30 percent times $2400).

LOSER: Residential Energy Credit.

Under the old law this credit equaled 15 percent of the first $2000 (for a maximum of $300) you spent installing insulation, storm windows, and other energy-saving products in your home. Intended to encourage homeowners to take steps to make their homes more energy-efficient, this credit expired in 1985 and was not renewed by the new tax law.

CHAPTER 13

FOREIGN AFFAIRS
Congress Tightens Expatriate Tax Incentives

CHANGES AT A GLANCE

Old Law	New Law
Americans who work abroad may exclude up to $80,000 of their earned income each year from taxation in the U.S.	Earned-income exclusion is reduced to $70,000 a year

Back in 1981 Congress did a favor for U.S. taxpayers who work abroad. It voted to boost the so-called earned-income exclusion.

These expatriate taxpayers were entitled to omit a big chunk of their earned income—up to $80,000 a year—from taxation in the United States. Amounts in excess of the earned-income exclusion were taxed at graduated rates as if the excess were the only income earned by the taxpayer. In addition, the U.S. laws allow a portion of foreign taxes paid by expatriates to be credited against—or subtracted from—their U.S. taxes.

The Tax Reform Act keeps most of these rules in place. But it rolls back the benefits of the foreign exclusion by reducing the amount of earned income expatriates may omit from U.S. taxation. The new ceiling is $70,000 a year.

AT A MINIMUM   As under the old law, taxpayers who pay the alternative minimum tax (AMT) may reduce it by any foreign tax credits they claim. The AMT is paid by individuals who, by taking advantage of various tax breaks, would otherwise pay little or no income tax despite their high incomes. The law requires you to pay the alternative minimum tax if it exceeds the amount you would owe Uncle Sam as determined under the regular income tax system.

As you'll see in the next chapter, Congress made substantial changes in the alternative minimum tax when it adopted the Tax Reform Act. Among them: No more than 90 percent of the tax liability computed under the AMT system, before credits, may be offset by foreign tax credits. This rule, in effect, prevents the AMT from ever reaching zero—although it may get close.

LET'S KEEP IN TOUCH   Too many expatriates, Congress says, fail to file U.S. income tax returns. So, the legislators found a way to identify some offenders.

The new tax law mandates that any person who seeks a United States passport must file an IRS information return with his or her passport application. A similar form must be filed by resident aliens when they apply for their green cards.

THE LAST WORD   The Tax Reform Act also requires that employers withhold income taxes from pension and annuity payments sent to people overseas. The only way around this rule: The recipient of the payment must certify that he or she is not a U.S. citizen or resident living overseas.

In addition, U.S. taxpayers who work in countries where they are not allowed—Libya, for example—may not exclude a cent of their income from U.S. taxation.

CHAPTER 14

NO ALTERNATIVE
Why More People Will Pay the Alternative Minimum Tax

CHANGES AT A GLANCE

Old Law	New Law
Taxpayers are subject to a 20-percent minimum tax	Taxpayers are subject to a 21-percent minimum tax
	Computational changes are made, and new concepts (deferral preferences and minimum tax credit) are introduced

A person may have very low—or even no—income to report on his or her tax return and still make plenty of money.

An individual, for example, who chalked up a $40,000 long-term capital gain in 1986 paid 30 percent less in income tax than a person who took home $40,000 a year from his or her job. Likewise, people who invest in tax shelters or claim substantial deductions or credits sometimes reduce taxable income to the vanishing point.

These are the taxpayers for whom the alternative minimum tax system (AMT) was invented. The idea behind the AMT is that everyone should pay his or her fair share of tax.

As a concept, the AMT is simple enough: It is a flat tax of 21 percent—20 percent under the old law—that is applied to more of your income than the regular income tax. The reason: Your income isn't reduced by as many deductions. Just as in the past, you calculate the minimum tax separately and pay it only when it exceeds your regular income tax.

Besides the increase in the AMT rate from 20 percent to 21 percent, the new law makes another significant change: The income base to which the rate applies—dubbed Alternative Minimum Taxable Income (AMTI)—is determined differently.

IT AIN'T EASY   While the AMT system sounds simple, understanding the rules and making the calculations can be a nightmare of complexity. And absolutely nothing in the new tax law makes the AMT any easier to deal with than it was under the old law.

If anything, the new rules and computations are even more difficult to understand than the old ones. Nonetheless, it's the law we have to live with, and so it's worth understanding, if only because understanding it may save you money.

WHO NEEDS TO KNOW?   The only way to know if you're subject to the alternative minimum tax is to put pencil to paper and "run the numbers."

Three changes in the new law mean that more taxpayers than ever before will be caught in the AMT web. These changes are:

• The treatment of losses from passive investments, such as tax shelters, during the phase-in period. These losses, which you may take for regular tax purposes, must be added back to taxable income when you figure the amount of your income subject to the alternative minimum tax.

• The narrowing of the difference between regular rates— 15 percent and 28 percent in 1988—and the AMT rate—21 percent. The old law provided for a much greater spread between the minimum and regular rates. The 1986 AMT rate, for example, is 40 percent of the top marginal rate. Starting in 1988 the AMT rate is 75 percent of the top tax bracket (an AMT rate of 21 percent divided by the top rate of 28 percent).

• The expansion of items that must be added back to income when figuring your alternative minimum tax. More income will be subject to the AMT bite.

DEFINING ALTERNATIVE MINIMUM TAXABLE INCOME

The amount of your income subject to the AMT is figured this way: You adjust your regular taxable income to reflect different AMT treatment of certain items.

Here's a checklist of the more common ones:

• Depreciation on real and personal property placed in service after 1986.

• Gain on the sale of assets depreciated differently for AMT purposes than for regular tax purposes—but only for assets placed in service after 1986.

• Losses from passive activity investments, such as tax shelters.

These adjustments, new under tax reform, permit you to either increase or decrease your income subject to the AMT. This "netting concept" is a victory of sorts for taxpayers, since it recognizes that most incentives the AMT is trying to curb only defer regular tax.

These adjustments differ from tax preferences under both the old law and the new—we discuss tax preferences below—since they can either be your friend or foe. Tax preferences always work against you.

The most important of the new adjustments: Depreciation and passive activity losses.

Depreciation. You must either increase or decrease your regular taxable income by the "net" difference between: depreciation figured using the Accelerated Cost Recovery System (ACRS); and depreciation figured using the alternative depreciation method. The provision applies to property placed in service after 1986.

Passive activity investments. During the four-year phase-in period beginning in 1987, you can use a certain percentage of your passive activity or tax shelter losses to offset your earned income and portfolio income for regular tax purposes. (See Chapter 5.)

But you can't use these losses to offset earned income and portfolio income when you compute AMTI. You may carry forward a passive activity loss and treat it as a deduction when you have AMTI net passive activity income in succeeding taxable years.

In addition, when you dispose of your entire interest in a tax shelter, you can use any carryovers that result from the denial of the phase-in loss to compute AMTI.

Besides the adjustments we've already discussed, you must also increase your regular taxable income for the more common tax preference items. These include:

- Itemized deductions not deductible for AMT, such as state and local income taxes, real estate taxes, medical expenses not greater than 10 percent of your AGI, and miscellaneous deductions—tax preparation fees and professional dues, for instance—to the extent that they exceed 2 percent of AGI. Also, all interest expense, except home mortgage interest and investment interest to the extent of net investment income, is not deductible for AMT.

Two points need to be made about the interest deduction for AMT: First, the phase-in rule for investment interest for regular tax purposes is disregarded for AMT purposes. (See Chapter 2.) Second, if you refinance your home mortgage, only interest on the refinanced mortgage equal to the debt before you refinanced will be allowed for AMT purposes. Thus, if you refinance your mortgage to avoid the new personal interest rules, this new AMT provision will deny the increased interest deduction in computing income subject to the AMT.

- Excess of the fair-market value over the purchase price—the so-called bargain element—of stock acquired when you exercise an incentive stock option (ISO). This excess becomes part of the stock's basis, so that when the stock is sold, the gain for AMT purposes will be less than the gain for regular tax purposes. (See Chapter 11.)

- Excess of accelerated depreciation over straight-line depreciation on real property and leased personal property placed in service before 1987.

- Excess of percentage depletion over the tax basis of the property generating the mineral deposit subject to depletion.

- Excess intangible drilling costs incurred in connection with productive oil and gas wells over 65 percent of the net income from these properties.

- Interest on certain tax-exempt bonds issued generally after August 7, 1986. This preference item only applies to "nonessential bonds," which generally represents bonds issued by state or local governments, where the proceeds of the bond issue are being used by private enterprise—for example, IDB's used by small businesses for plant and building needs.

• Excess of the value of property contributed to a charitable organization and deducted for regular tax purposes as an itemized deduction over the cost of such property.

• Excess research and experimentation expenditures over the amount deductible if amortized over a ten-year period.

ADJUSTING AMTI   When you've made all the required adjustments to your regular taxable income, and accounted for all tax preference items, the net sum is your AMTI. Now, the law says, you may reduce it by the following standard exemptions: $40,000 for taxpayers filing a joint return, and $30,000 for single taxpayers.

However, if your AMTI is high—in the eyes of Uncle Sam—the new law reduces your exemption. The exemption is reduced by 25 percent of the amount by which AMTI exceeds $150,000 for married taxpayers filing jointly ($112,500 for single filers).

NOT QUITE COMPUTING YOUR TAX   Once you've adjusted your AMTI by the appropriate exemption, if any, then multiply it by 21 percent. The result—after subtracting allowable foreign tax credits—is called your tentative minimum tax (TMT).

The foreign tax credit offset is now limited to 90 percent of TMT before the foreign tax credit.

Compare the TMT to your regular tax. If your TMT is larger, the excess is the alternative minimum tax, which you must pay in addition to your regular tax.

But you may not yet have completed the whole calculation of your tax liability. Another item, called a minimum tax credit (MTC), may work to your advantage in future years. Figuring MTC is easier if you understand a few of the concepts that Congress has incorporated into the new alternative minimum tax provisions.

WHAT'S BEHIND MTC   The adjustments that you have made thus far to your regular taxable income in order to compute AMTI fall into one of two categories. Either they are ''deferral preferences'' or ''exclusion preferences.''

Deferral preferences are, in a sense, the good news in the revised AMT rules Congress has written. The lawmakers acknowledge that the adjustments and preferences that fall into this category don't permanently reduce anyone's tax liability. They only defer that liability until some later time.

Only four items—the percentage-depletion preference, the itemized-deduction items, the appreciated-property charitable-contribution preference item, and the tax-exempt preference item—fall outside the deferral preference category. These items are called exclusion preferences.

The government never recaptures the tax revenue lost when a taxpayer reduces his or her liability by using an exclusion preference. That is, the deductions taken for these items do not represent an acceleration of a deduction (for example, ACRS depreciation) or the deferral of income (for example, the fact that although your wealth has increased on the exercise of an ISO, this wealth is not taxed until the stock is sold).

Rather, when a taxpayer takes a deduction for these items, it is a one-time deduction, and it is final. Nothing that occurs in the future will have any impact on the deduction taken in the current year.

Thus, the MTC, which may reduce your tax liability in future years, is a recognition of the difference between these two kinds of preferences. MTC represents the total AMT paid reduced by the amount of AMT that would have been paid if you had only counted exclusion preferences.

You may carry forward this amount indefinitely (although you may not carry it back) as an offset against future years' regular tax liabilities. The regular tax, however, can be reduced only to an amount equal to the TMT in the respective carryforward year.

THE LAST WORD Those who can manage the timing of income, deductions, and occurrences of originating and reversing AMT adjustments and preferences will be in the best position to save tax dollars under the new AMT rules.

Since individuals will now be more susceptible to the AMT, it will be necessary to project the consequences of tax strategies under the regular tax and AMT in order that tax savings from the strategies are not diluted by the AMT.

CHAPTER 15

THE BIG PICTURE
Creating a Winning Tax Plan
for 1986 and Beyond

It's a national pastime that begins after Labor Day, just as your favorite halfback dashes into the end zone for his first touchdown.

The fans rise to their feet cheering, but there's something else lurking in the back of their minds: It's time for year-end tax planning. It's the season to sidestep a hard tackle by Uncle Sam.

But what strategies should you follow now that tax reform is upon us? Here's our checklist of winning tax strategies—not only for 1986 but for 1987 and beyond.

INDIVIDUAL TAX PLANNING FOR 1986 The lower rates mandated by the new law mean that most people will benefit from time-honored, year-end tax planning strategies. These tactics—defer income and accelerate deductions—made sense before tax reform. But the new law makes them even more effective for the following two reasons.

First, the tax deferred until 1987 generates a time value of money benefit—that is, you get to keep your money longer. Second, by deferring taxable income from 1986 to 1987, most filers will pay taxes on that income at a lower rate. Conversely, accelerating deductions into 1986 makes good sense, since that year's higher rates makes the deductions more valuable. So, this strategy yields permanent tax savings as well as a temporary cash flow benefit.

Still, "most people" doesn't include everyone. Say, for instance, that your 1986 taxable income is abnormally low, because your employer failed to pay a customary bonus, or your deductions and losses were abnormally high, substantially reducing your taxable income.

For you, the opposite tactic might work best. It might be more effective to accelerate income into 1986 and defer paying deductible expenses until 1987. The only way to identify the right strategy is to crunch the numbers: Most of the clicking of calculator buttons over the next few months will concern the deferral or acceleration of income and deductions. That's where the average taxpayer can realize significant savings.

Following are some specific strategies to consider. Keep in mind, though, that many of these tactics are dependent on whether it's a good idea—for nontax reasons—for you to defer income or accelerate deductions.

STRATEGY: Postpone Receipt of Earned Income

If you're employed by someone else, defer receipt of your salary, bonus, or commissions. If you work for yourself, postpone billing clients or customers until near the end of the year, so payment is received after January 1.

Caveat: Take care that you don't become ensnared by the "constructive receipt" rules. These rules apply when you have an unrestricted right to receive income and it is available to you.

Say you've knocked yourself out for your employer, and he plans to pay you a bonus in 1986. He tells you that you may collect your bonus on December 31, 1986. Even if you decide not to pick up the check until January 2, 1987, you have to declare the bonus amount as taxable income in 1986.

To get around this rule, you must choose to defer compensation before you earn it—that is, before you perform the services. For example, to postpone receiving income on services you will provide during the last two and one-half months of 1986, you must decide—before October 15—to defer the income. And you must have a written agreement that describes you as a general creditor of your employer. This contract is called a "nonqualified deferred compensation agreement."

Also, the IRS says your election must be irrevocable—that is, you can't later decide that you want part of what's coming to you in 1986 without jeopardizing the deferral of the whole amount. You must be able to convince the IRS that you were not entitled to the salary until after 1986.

STRATEGY: Defer Interest Income

Purchase financial instruments—Certificates of Deposit, Treasury Bills, U.S. Savings Bonds, and so on—maturing in 1987 and beyond. Under the law you don't have to pay taxes on the interest these investments earn until they mature.

Another idea: If you own U.S. Savings Bonds maturing in 1986, keep the bonds beyond their maturity date or make a tax-free exchange of your U.S. bonds for another nontransferable U.S. obligation. That way, you defer reporting the interest as income.

STRATEGY: Defer Dividend Income

It's not easy to do. But you can petition the board of directors of a corporation in which you are a shareholder to postpone a 1986 dividend until the following year. This tactic, of course, will work only if you own a significant percentage of the stock.

STRATEGY: Defer Receipt of Employee Benefits

If you withdraw money from a qualified pension or profit-sharing plan in 1986, you may avoid paying taxes on it immediately.

Just roll it over to an IRA or another type of qualified retirement plan within sixty days. You will not be taxed until you subsequently withdraw the funds.

But beware: Favorable ten-year forward-averaging provisions do not apply to distributions from IRA's, even if the amount rolled into the IRA would have qualified for forward averaging when it was distributed.

STRATEGY: Take "Last-Chance" Deductions

Cash in on the vanishing sales tax deduction by purchasing big-ticket items, such as a boat, furniture, or a car, by the end of 1986. Also, don't forget to look at actual expenditures when figuring up your 1986 sales tax deduction.

The charitable deduction for those who do not itemize will no longer be available after 1986. Nonitemizers should accelerate contributions into 1986 so they may still write them off.

Itemizers should also accelerate charitable deductions. You might consider making lump-sum contributions in 1986 that would replace some or all of the periodic contributions you expect to make in 1987. These might include weekly church contributions or charitable contributions withheld from your paycheck. This strategy holds true for all contributions you expect to make in the future.

If you are considering making a gift of appreciated property, such as stock, to a charity, not only would you enjoy the tax benefits generally associated with a 1986 gift, but you would avoid the alternative minimum tax that may be imposed on a 1987 contribution of appreciated property. (See Chapter 14.)

You may be able to accelerate years of charitable contributions into 1986 by establishing a grantor charitable lead trust in 1986. To obtain a current income tax deduction, the charitable lead trust must qualify as a "grantor trust." To qualify, the trust must generally be created for a term not in excess of ten years, with the trust funds returned to the donor upon termination of the trust. This approach may be valuable if a substantial income tax deduction is desired in one particular year—1986, for instance. However, the grantor trust rules are restrictive and should be cautiously considered.

Under the grantor trust provisions, the donor is treated as the substantial owner and must include all items of trust income on his or her personal return. Although the grantor may receive an immediate charitable deduction for the present value of the income stream, the deduction is limited to 30 percent of the donor's adjusted gross income (AGI). In future years, however, the donor must include the trust income on his or her personal return—probably at lower rates—without a corresponding deduction.

STRATEGY: Accelerate Miscellaneous Deductions

In 1987 these expenses are deductible to the extent they exceed 2 percent of your adjusted gross income. (See Chapter 3.) These expenses include the cost of continuing education, subscriptions to professional journals, and professional dues. Also on the list: the cost of job hunting, investment adviser and management fees, tax preparation and advisory fees, and safe deposit box charges.

STRATEGY: Accelerate T&E Deductions

Better to entertain in 1986 than in 1987 because only 80 percent of the costs will be deductible in 1987. And these deductions will be worth less because of the lowering of the rates. So throw a December holiday party instead of a Super Bowl party for your customers and clients.

STRATEGY: Speed Up Payment of Medical Expenses

In 1986 you may write off medical expenses that exceed 5 percent of your adjusted gross income. In 1987 the 5-percent floor jumps to 7.5 percent.

If you've already topped the 5-percent mark for 1986, pay any of your outstanding medical bills before year-end or hold off filing medical reimbursement claims to defer reimbursement until 1987. Net expenses over the 5-percent floor are fully deductible.

If you're self-employed, though, you should defer medical insurance payments, since the new tax law allows you to subtract one-quarter of your health insurance premiums from your taxable income. The old law doesn't permit this deduction.

STRATEGY: Prepay State and Local Taxes

If you pay estimated state taxes, make your fourth quarterly payment, normally due in January 1987, before the end of 1986. And if there's a chance you'll owe money when you file your local or state tax returns, authorize your employer to increase the amount of tax withheld for the rest of the year. Or, if you make estimated tax payments, send the state or local department of revenue a check for the estimated balance due in 1986 rather than paying when you file your returns in April 1987.

But don't be greedy. Keep your state income tax prepayment reasonable to avoid challenge by the IRS.

STRATEGY: Accelerate Purchase of a New Home

If possible, close on the purchase of a new home by year-end. Doing so will accelerate the deduction of points incurred on your new mortgage and your share of the real estate taxes.

STRATEGY: Pay Up Interest Charges by Year-End

To the extent possible, you should pay the interest expenses that have accrued for 1986—such as the December interest costs on your home mortgage—before 1987.

Also, check your lender's 1986 statement regarding interest to make sure that all interest paid in 1986 was reported.

STRATEGY: Cut Back on Personal Interest

Uncle Sam won't wholly subsidize interest payments on your car or refrigerator anymore. So try to reduce the interest you pay on personal loans and credit cards after 1986.

The deduction for personal interest is phased out gradually

over the next four years: In 1987 you may write off only 65 percent of your personal interest. By 1991 you may write off none. (See Chapter 2.)

You may be able to sidestep the personal interest limitation by tapping the equity in your house. Mortgage interest is still fully deductible.

So consider refinancing the mortgage on your first or second home. With the interest rates now relatively low, this may be the appropriate time to refinance. But remember, you may refinance only up to the original purchase price plus the cost of improvements—unless the excess is used for medical or educational purposes.

Assume you bought your home in 1982 for $89,000 and put in another $6000 for improvements. You can borrow up to $95,000 and the interest will be fully deductible. Once you refinance, use the available funds to pay off outstanding auto loans and credit card balances or other personal debt.

But beware: There are costs associated with refinancing—points, appraisal fees, and title costs—that detract from this tax-planning opportunity. (Note that the IRS has indicated that points on refinancing must be deducted over the life of the loan, rather than in the year you pay them.)

Another potential trap: The interest on a refinancing may result in a partial disallowance of the interest deduction for alternative minimum tax purposes. (See Chapter 14.)

STRATEGY: Take Stock of Capital Gains and Losses

You've heard it before. And you'll hear it again. Every investor should take a second look at his or her portfolio with an eye to the changes wrought by the Tax Reform Act of 1986.

The new law zaps the favorable treatment of long-term capital gains. Investors may no longer exclude 60 percent of their long-term gains from taxation. So the top tax on long-term capital gains increases from 20 percent to 28 percent in 1987. And if you're in a bracket lower than 50 percent, the difference is even greater.

Our advice: If you're considering selling a stock or bond you've held for more than six months, do so in 1986—not 1987—to cash in on capital-gain treatment.

Under the new tax law, you also lose the option of deferring the gain on year-end sales of stocks and bonds. You have this option in 1986 though. To qualify, your trade date and settlement date must straddle the year-end—that is, you sell the stock, say, on December 28 (trade date) and receive the proceeds on January 2 (settlement date).

This option provides you with "hindsight" planning opportunities. It allows you to wait until the due date of your 1986 return to decide whether to recognize the gain in 1986 or 1987.

Say you score big, on paper, on a stock and want to take advantage of the lower capital-gain tax for 1986. But you still think the stock has some life in it, and you're reluctant to sell.

Here's a way to satisfy both inclinations: After selling the stock, you can repurchase it. By doing so, you increase the tax basis to current market value.

The price you pay under this approach: You will incur additional transaction costs—commissions and transfer taxes—and accelerate the payment of tax.

If you are in the later years of your life and believe that you may hold on to the stock until death, then you do not want to sell it in 1986 to lock in the long-term capital-gain deduction. That's because appreciation on property held at the time of death is not subject to income taxes, and the tax basis of the property is stepped up to its fair market value at the time of death. Consequently, the appreciation in the stock would not be subject to income taxes if held until death.

The new law leaves in place the $3000 cap on deduction for capital losses. But it also lets you deduct long-term capital losses on a dollar-for-dollar basis. Under the old rules you could deduct only 50 cents of each dollar you lost.

The elimination of the 50-percent limitation on long-term capital losses could result in the permanent loss of up to $3000 if you sold in 1986 versus 1987. (Of course, this scenario assumes no other gains in 1986.) This provision, though, may not make enough of a difference to stop you from unloading a real loser in 1986. But the capital-loss deduction—after 1986—is worth less because of the lower rates.

What about short-term capital gains and losses? If possible, defer short-term capital gains until next year. Here's why: In 1986 these gains are subject to a maximum tax of 50 percent. In 1987 the ceiling is 38.5 percent.

On the other hand it's best to take short-term losses in 1986, when higher tax rates make the deduction worth more. But make sure the short-term losses you accelerate to 1986 do not offset long-term capital gains. If you do not have long-term gains, do not accelerate losses in excess of $3000. If you do, you will be subject to the $3000 loss limitation.

Installment sales have also undergone changes under the new law. When you sell a capital asset, such as a piece of land, payments are often received over a number of years. That way you defer recognition of the capital gain—and delay paying the tax. But under the new law, sellers will lose the favorable long-term capital-gain deduction on installment payments that are made after 1986.

If this new rule affects you, you may want to arrange in 1986 for prepayment of the note, "sell" it to a third party—such as a financial or lending institution—or exchange it for other property. When you do, the remaining gain is accelerated and taxed in 1986 when the more favorable capital-gain rules apply.

Make sure, though, that you examine the downside of this strategy. For example, you most likely will receive less cash than if you held the note to maturity.

STRATEGY: Generate Passive Activity Income

Starting in 1987 you may no longer use "passive losses" from tax shelters to offset income from wages, salary, interest, and dividends. You may deduct them only from passive activity income—until the activity is disposed of in a taxable transaction.

If you've invested in tax shelters still generating losses, you may want to invest in a profitable general partnership or small company that is—or is planning to become—an S corporation. Often, small businesses are looking for additional capital. But you must restrict your role to that of investor only. (Remember, passive activity means you do not "materially participate" in the management of a trade or business.)

Any operating net income generated from the S corporation and passed through to you is considered passive activity income. Another benefit: Any portfolio income from your investment—interest, dividends, and so on—is treated as investment income and increases your investment interest expense limitation.

STRATEGY: Investigate Remaining Real Estate Opportunities

The next few months may be an ideal time to buy that apartment building you've wanted. Mortgage rates are still very favorable, and property that you purchase before 1987 locks in the benefit of more generous depreciation provisions.

But take heed: The $25,000 cap on the deduction for rental

property losses declines on a two-for-one basis for taxpayers with adjusted gross income over $100,000. So you can't take losses if your AGI is more than $150,000.

Due to the AGI phase-out and the $25,000 cap on rental losses, careful planning related to the timing of income recognition and deductions is necessary to realize the maximum benefit of your rental losses year after year.

STRATEGY: Cash In on the Highs of Low-Income Housing Credits

Consider investing in low-income housing or real property rehabilitation projects. Why? The credits available from these activities (see Chapter 19) are treated as arising from real estate rental activities in which you actively participate. As a result they are two of the only activities left intact under the new law where you can limit your liability and your participation—for example, by investing as a limited partner or S corporation shareholder—and still be able to offset nonpassive income. Credits (but not losses) from these activities may be used to offset tax on up to $25,000 of nonpassive income. In addition the AGI phase-out is higher: from $200,000 to $250,000.

Be careful though. It is not uncommon for either of these activities to have negative pre-tax cash flow and operating losses. This is because rental income is often not sufficient to cover operating expenses and debt service. Since the losses will be subject to the passive activity rules, you must weigh carefully both the economic and tax advantages and disadvantages.

STRATEGY: Zero In on Oil and Gas Properties

You still may reap tax benefits by investing in oil and gas properties. Lawmakers made an exception to the new tax shelter rules for working interests in oil and gas properties. So you're not subject to the new harsh passive loss rules.

Moreover, the beneficial percentage depletion provisions were not changed by the new tax law. Careful evaluation of the economics of an oil and gas investment must be made in light of current market conditions.

STRATEGY: Size Up Tax-Exempt Bonds

Because of the new passive activity rules and the current favorable tax-exempt bond market, you should consider this type of investment as a "new tax-advantaged" vehicle.

STRATEGY: Be Wary of the Alternative Minimum Tax Bite

The new law modifies the alternative minimum tax (AMT) provisions by broadening the income base. In addition the compression of the tax rates will subject more taxpayers to the AMT bite. Before tax planning strategies are implemented, you must assess the impact of the AMT, so that the benefit of the strategy is not diluted.

STRATEGY: Take Stock of Income-Shifting Options

The new law scales back the benefits of transferring income-producing assets to a minor child. Now, net unearned income that children under fourteen receive is taxed at the child's or parent's tax rate, whichever is higher.

This provision is retroactive: Money or property you gave to a child under fourteen—even if the assets were received by the child before 1987—will be subject to the new rules. Moreover, the law specifically forbids the use of short-term trusts, such as the popular Clifford trust or spousal-remainder trust, as income-shifting devices. Now, income and deductions generated by these trusts are considered part of the grantor's taxable income—not the beneficiary's.

The new rules apply to transfers made to a trust after March 1, 1986. Transfers to a trust before that date still operate under the favorable old law—that is, the income is taxed at either the beneficiary's or trust's lower rate.

The income-shifting game isn't entirely over, however. You can still pursue several income-shifting strategies. For one, you can give your children money to acquire U.S. Savings Bonds or to purchase an annuity from, say, an insurance company. Similarly, it's a good idea to give appreciating assets, such as growth stocks, to young children. The appreciation won't be taxed until the asset is sold or the annuity payments begin. If the sale occurs after the child's fourteenth birthday, the capital gain will be taxed at the child's lower rates.

Remember, generally the first $1000 of net unearned income is taxed at the child's lower rates. Therefore, you should consider structuring your child's investments so that he or she recognizes only $1000 of net unearned income in a given year, with any excess deferred until he or she reaches fourteen.

Shifting income to children over fourteen still makes good sense. So consider establishing a savings account or stock portfolio in your child's name to help accumulate savings for a college education.

These new rules on income-shifting won't affect employing your children in a family business. In fact, the child may use his or her standard deduction to shelter up to $3000 of earned income in 1988.

And if you need to tap the equity in your home—up to the fair market value—to send your son or daughter to college, go ahead. You won't be able to deduct the interest you pay on an outside student loan, but you may deduct your mortgage interest. But beware of the AMT bite discussed above.

STRATEGY: Make the Most of IRA's and 401(k)s

Beginning in 1987 you can't deduct your IRA contributions if you are an active participant in another qualified retirement plan. (You're excepted from this rule if your adjusted gross income is not more than $40,000 for married couples filing jointly and $25,000 for single taxpayers. But this exception is gradually phased out as your income climbs. Joint filers with an AGI of $50,000 or more and single filers with $35,000 or more may not make deductible contributions.)

You have until April 15, 1987, to make your IRA contribution for 1986—so take advantage while you still can. Lawmakers also placed tough restrictions on the increasingly popular 401(k) plans, which enable employees to defer taxes on a portion of their salary. Beginning in 1987 you face a $7000 limitation on the amount of pre-tax compensation you may defer. You may still increase your contribution for the balance of 1986, however, if your employer's plan allows it. This year you may accumulate up to $30,000.

Don't be too aggressive though. It will cost you dearly to withdraw the money before you retire or reach age fifty-nine and one-half.

If you cannot make deductible IRA contributions, you might consider making nondeductible contributions, since the earnings still accumulate tax-free until withdrawn. However, remember early withdrawals—except for the nondeductible contributions— are subject to the 10-percent penalty in addition to tax. And these nondeductible contributions become part of the total IRA "pool" and may be withdrawn on a pro rata basis only.

When evaluating your decision, consider after-tax returns on other non-IRA investments—such as tax-exempt bonds, growth stocks, etc.—not subject to withdrawal penalties and tax (in the case of tax-exempt bonds).

If you have a choice, you might consider first investing in a 401(k) plan with pre-tax dollars—up to the $7000 maximum.

This is cheaper to fund than nondeductible IRA contributions since you are using pre-tax dollars. And earnings accumulate tax-free until withdrawn.

Also, loans are permissible from 401(k) plans—but not IRA's. (See Chapters 9 and 10.)

What if you needed money to pay the college tuition bill for your daughter? You could borrow from your 401(k) plan. But you cannot borrow from your IRA. Loans from IRA's are considered distributions subject to tax and perhaps the 10-percent premature withdrawal penalty. And hardship withdrawals (although tightened by tax reform) are allowed from 401(k) plans, but not from IRA's.

The new law also dramatically changes the taxation of lump-sum distributions. After 1986 many people will no longer have the benefit of ten-year-averaging. You lose out on other favorable rules too. Some taxpayers may no longer take distributions before retirement, for instance.

So if you are nearing retirement, it might be a good idea to take your distribution in 1986, rather than wait until 1987.

STRATEGY: For Those "Untying the Knot"—Beware

If you're separated and the parent of a child, take note: Congress turned personal exemption tax planning rules upside down.

In the past it made sense for the higher-income parent to claim the child as a dependent, because the exemption was worth more to that parent. But starting in 1988 only the lower-income parent may benefit from the personal exemption deduction. That's because after 1987 the tax benefits of the personal exemptions you claim for your child and yourself are phased out as your income increases.

Other considerations for couples filing for divorce: The new law still allows people to deduct the alimony payments they make. It also requires the recipient of alimony to report this amount as income to Uncle Sam.

But the reduction in the tax rates from 50 percent to 28 percent will make alimony more costly to the spouse who makes these payments. Uncle Sam will no longer subsidize 50 percent, but only 28 percent—a change that could lead to more reliance on property settlements.

But with the elimination of favorable treatment of capital

gains, these settlements may prove to be more costly. Transfers of appreciated property are not taxable until the property is sold.

Under the old law the spouse who received the property paid tax on the gain at a rate of only 13 percent, if he or she had, say, a 33-percent top bracket.

Under the new law, the gain would be taxed at 28 percent. Thus, the recipient in a property settlement will be better off taking cash than appreciated property. Or, conversely, consider the increased capital-gain tax when negotiating your settlement.

INDIVIDUAL TAX PLANNING FOR 1987 AND BEYOND

The new lower tax rates are fully effective in 1988. So the basic acceleration and deferral planning ideas we've discussed are still applicable when planning your 1987 tax affairs.

What about capital gains? You pay up to 38.5 percent tax on short-term gains in 1987, versus 28 percent—or 33 percent, in some cases—in 1988. The 28-percent cap on gains in 1987 is limited to net capital gains—that is, net long-term gains over net short-term gains. So if you have short-term and long-term gains in 1987, only the long-term gains are capped at 28 percent. The short-term gains could be taxed at up to 38.5 percent in 1987, but only 28 or 33 percent in 1988. Thus, defer these short-term gains until 1988.

Depending on your taxable income in 1988, long-term capital gains may be taxed at 33 percent in 1988. If this is the case, accelerating a long-term capital gain into 1987 may make sense.

THE LAST WORD   As a general rule you may deduct an expense in the year you pay it whether the amount was due or not. But the law won't allow you to prepay certain items. In general the law prohibits advance payments that "would materially distort taxable income."

We suggest that before you make an advance payment you ask yourself two key questions: Is prepayment advisable, considering my financial condition and the income I'll lose on the prepaid money? Will my payees accept early payment? If the answer to these two questions is "yes," accelerate the deductions to 1986.

In case you didn't know: If you use your credit cards to pay for expenses near year-end, you qualify for a current-year deduction even though you don't pay the bill until the next year.

PART 2

THE COMING CRACKDOWN

CHAPTER 16

NO MORE MR. NICE GUY
Congress Flexes Its Muscles

CHANGES AT A GLANCE

Old Law	New Law
The IRS imposes the same interest rate on tax underpayments as on tax overpayments	The IRS charges one percent more on underpayments than it pays on overpayments
The IRS has no authority to abate interest charges	The IRS authorized to abate interest charges if the interest stems from an IRS error
Negligence penalty equals 5 percent of total underpayment plus interest component; fraud penalty equal to 50 percent of underpayment plus interest component	Negligence penalty is assessed on underpayment not attributable to fraud; fraud penalty is increased to 75 percent of underpayment attributable to fraud
Taxpayers aren't required to report real estate transactions to the IRS	Real estate transactions must be reported to the IRS

What good is a tax law without sharp teeth? What good is a penalty that adds up to significantly less than the violation it is supposed to punish?

Not much, thought the authors of the Tax Reform Act.

So while they were reducing tax rates, eliminating deductions, and chopping tax credits, they also tightened some rules and hiked some penalties. The idea was to encourage taxpayer compliance with the Internal Revenue Code by making noncompliance harder to hide and more expensive when discovered.

In this chapter we summarize the changes.

NOT IN YOUR INTEREST   Sometimes you borrow from the IRS. Sometimes the IRS borrows from you. Often the borrowing is inadvertent, but deliberate or not, interest must be paid. The new law changes the interest rates that will apply.

Formerly, it didn't matter, as far as interest rates were concerned, whether you owed the IRS because of underpayment or the IRS owed you because of overpayment. Whoever owed whom, the interest rate levied on the outstanding balance was the same. It was pegged to prime lending rates and was adjusted semiannually.

The new tax law gives Uncle Sam a one-percent break. For tax years starting after 1986, the interest the IRS pays on an overpayment will be adjusted quarterly and will be based on the federal short-term rate—the average market yields of Treasury Bills and other U.S. obligations with terms of three years or less. The IRS will pay this rate plus 2 percent on overpayments. You, however, will be charged the federal short-term rate plus 3 percent on underpayments.

Sound fair? Maybe not, but few banks borrow and lend at the same interest rates. And Uncle Sam didn't think it should have to either.

PLAYING YOUR CARDS TOO CLOSE TO YOUR VEST

Uncle Sam doesn't want a corporation to hold on to more of its earnings than is necessary to meet its needs. He wants profits in excess of the company's needs paid out as dividends to stockholders. So money is taxed twice—once at the corporate level as corporate earnings, then again as dividends to shareholders.

Corporations that on audit are found guilty of holding on to too much of their cash are slapped with an accumulated earnings tax. Basically the tax may be assessed if your accumulated earnings exceed $250,000, the amount Uncle Sam says is reasonable to meet your needs, unless you prove otherwise.

The tax, which is paid in addition to normal corporate income taxes, equals 27.5 percent of the first $100,000 of accumulated earnings in excess of $250,000 and 38.5 percent of the remainder.

Under the old law the IRS didn't impose interest on amounts it designated as accumulated earnings until it got around to demanding you pay up. Now interest charges on accumulated earnings begin on the due date of the return—not including extensions—in the year for which the tax is imposed.

EVERYONE MAKES MISTAKES   Even when it was willing to admit that a taxpayer had gotten hit with an interest charge because of an IRS mistake, the agency had no authority to reduce or forgive the charge.

The new tax law, however, gives the agency authority to forgive the charge when an IRS official either fails to perform or makes an error in performing a procedure. It doesn't, however, say the agency has to. The matter is left up to IRS discretion, depending on the facts and circumstances of each case.

But the new law says the agency must—in cases of erroneous refunds of less than $50,000—abate, or forgive, the interest charge.

Suppose, for instance, that you filed a return and claimed a $200 refund, but the government sent you $2000 instead. Under the old law the IRS had to charge you interest on the $1800 difference for as long as you held the money—even though the fault was theirs. Now the interest will be abated.

This abatement provision applies to interest accruing on deficiencies or payments for taxable years beginning after 1978. The result: If you made interest payments to the IRS because of an agency mistake on your 1979 through 1985 returns, you may be able to secure a refund. Ask the IRS to abate the interest. You have nothing to lose—and a few dollars to gain.

NO REGRETS   To encourage people to comply with the tax code, Congress has modified many of the law's penalty provisions. As you might expect, most of these changes make the law rougher on the offender. The new rules become effective for tax returns due after 1986.

TIME FLIES   The new law modifies the monthly penalty for people who fail to pay their taxes either at the time they file their return or after they have received a notice for payment on a deficiency from the IRS. The penalty is one percent of the tax not paid—up from one-half of one percent normally—for each month the tax bill remains outstanding.

This increase kicks in, however, only after the IRS notifies you that it intends to levy your assets (usually ten days before they do so). Until you get the notice, the penalty stays at one-half of one percent. But once it kicks in, the penalty stays at one percent for all subsequent months.

However, the penalty cannot exceed 25 percent of the tax not paid. The penalty increases one percent (or one-half percent if you haven't received the levy notice from the IRS) for each additional month you don't pay.

YOU'RE NEGLECTING ME   Under the old law, if you negligently underpaid your taxes, you were subject to a penalty equal to 5 percent of your total underpayment—plus half of the interest due on the amount of the underpayment attributable to negligence. It didn't matter if only part of your underpayment was due to negligence or disregard of rules, the 5 percent was assessed on the total underpayment.

If you fraudulently underpaid your taxes, the IRS would slap you with a penalty equal to 50 percent of the underpayment plus half of the interest due on the portion attributable to fraud. If the underpayment involved both fraud and negligence, then only the higher fraud penalty was imposed.

For example, suppose, upon audit, an agent found that you underpaid your taxes for the year by $1000—$700 was due to an honest mistake (a math error), but $300 was due to a negligent, but not fraudulent, overstatement of your travel and entertainment expenses.

Under the old law the very existence of negligence meant that the entire underpayment of $1000 was subject to the negligence penalty of 5 percent, plus one half of the interest on $300. The new law stiffens the fraud and negligence penalties. But it also makes their application more fair. Here's the rundown:

• If you're found guilty of fraud, the penalty jumps from 50 percent to 75 percent of your underpayment. The interest component is unchanged. Also, the penalty now applies only to the amount of the tax underpayment due to fraud—not, as in the past, to the total amount of the underpayment. But the burden is on you to prove that the entire underpayment is not attributable to fraud. This change takes effect for tax years after 1986.

• The negligence penalty percentage remains unchanged. However, now it is assessed only on the part of the total tax underpayment not attributed to fraud. Suppose that your $1000 underpayment above was the result of a $200 math error, a $500 negligent overstatement of your travel expenses, and a $300 fraudulent omission of income. The 75-percent fraud penalty would be assessed on the $300 omission of income. Since you were negligent as well, you'd have to pay the 5-percent negligence penalty on the remaining $700 underpayment—the part not attributable to fraud—even though the $200 stemmed from an honest mistake.

• Also, under the new law the IRS treats your failure to include in your tax return any amount that was shown on an information return—a Form W-2 or 1099, for example—as automatic negligence. The result: You get zapped with a negligence penalty.

• In addition, the negligence penalty now applies to all taxes— from income taxes to estate taxes. Previously it applied only to income taxes, gift taxes, and the windfall profits tax.

INFORMATION PLEASE   The new law retains the $50 penalty currently imposed on businesses for each failure to file an information return with the IRS and for each failure to supply a copy of the information return to the taxpayer.

But after 1986 the maximum cumulative penalty a business can rack up for each category of multiple failures doubles—from $50,000 a year to $100,000. So a maximum penalty of $100,000 applies for failure to file with the IRS. And another $100,000 maximum penalty applies for failure to supply a copy to the taxpayer.

The law also adds a $5 penalty for each information return submitted to the IRS, or the taxpayer, that contains incorrect information. In most cases the maximum annual penalty here is $20,000.

GROSS UNDERSTATEMENT   Congress boosted the "substantial understatement" penalty from 10 percent to 20 percent of the tax understatement. Under the new law, you're guilty of substantial understatement when the amount of tax you show on your return falls short of the tax you should have listed by $5000—$10,000 for most corporations—or by 10 percent, whichever is greater.

Here's how it works: Imagine you're a salesperson and you spend money freely on travel and entertainment. Upon audit the agent informs you that she's disallowed most of your travel and entertainment deductions. What's worse, you owe Uncle Sam an additional $5500 in tax. Under the old law your penalty would total $550. Now it's $1100.

TAKE SHELTER   To deter both promoters and investors who skirt the laws of the Internal Revenue Code as it applies to tax shelters, Congress has significantly strengthened the penalty provisions of the old law.

The minimum penalty for failing to register a tax shelter with the IRS has remained the same, $500. Meanwhile, the maximum penalty increases from $10,000 to one percent of the total amount invested. Assume you're a promoter of a proposed equipment-leasing venture that meets the definition of a tax shelter. The total amount invested in the partnership is $2.5 million. If you fail to register the partnership as a tax shelter with the IRS, you will be penalized $25,000—$15,000 more than under the old law.

Second, Congress hiked the maximum penalty from $50,000 to $100,000 for failing to maintain lists of tax shelter investors. The penalty remains $50 per name omitted. Finally, the penalty for failing to report a tax shelter identification number on a tax return jumps from $50 to $250.

INFORMATION OVERLOAD   To help the IRS keep track of taxpayers' taxable transactions—and as a helpful reminder to you that these transactions are indeed taxable—the authors of the new law added some items to those already reportable to the agency and to taxpayers. Information called for under the new law is to be reported on Form 1099, just like the reports your bank files on your interest income and your broker files on your stock trades. Here are some of the new information reporting requirements.

• All real estate transactions closing after January 1, 1987—including the sale of a home of your own—must be reported on Form 1099. The primary reporting responsibility falls to the person responsible for closing the transaction—usually the settlement attorney or title company—if there is one. If there is no person responsible for closing the transaction, the primary mortgage lender, or the seller's broker, or the buyer's broker, in that order, must forward copies of Form 1099 to the buyer, seller, and IRS.

• The rules that say you must file a Form 1099 for interest and dividends now go for royalties too. This new reporting requirement applies to royalty payments made after 1986, if they come to $10 or more in any calendar year.

• Finally, the new law requires federal agencies to file information reports regarding their contracts. Agencies must report to the IRS the name, address, and Social Security or employer-identification number of each person contracting with them, effective January 1, 1986.

THE LAST WORD   Under the old law you do not have to report the amount of any tax-exempt interest income you received. After all, why would you report interest from, say, a municipal bond, when the interest isn't subject to taxation?

The problem, according to the lawmakers: The amount of tax-exempt interest you receive determines the amount of tax you pay in other areas. For example, tax-exempt interest earned on some bonds is used in figuring your alternative minimum tax liability. So starting in 1987 all taxpayers must disclose on their income tax returns the amount of tax-exempt income they receive.

CHAPTER 17

KEEPING UP
What You Should Now Know About Estimated Taxes

CHANGES AT A GLANCE

Old Law	New Law
Estimated tax payments equal 80 percent of current year's liability or 100 percent of last year's tax bill	Estimated tax payments equal 90 percent of current year's liability or 100 percent of last year's tax bill
Interest on money you borrow to pay taxes is deductible	Interest on money borrowed to pay taxes is subject to the new personal interest rules

With few exceptions every taxpayer must pay estimated tax to the Internal Revenue Service. These payments may take the form of taxes withheld from your paycheck. Or they may take the form of four quarterly installments sent by you to Uncle Sam.

STAND UP AND BE COUNTED　For most of us, paying our estimated tax is a relatively painless process, since we never actually see the cash. Our employers withhold it from our paychecks and forward it to Uncle Sam.

But taxpayers who don't have employers, and those with substantial income beyond their wages and salaries, have a bit of a problem. They have to make their own payments, including those for income and self-employment taxes—the equivalent of

Social Security—as well as for other tax liabilities, such as the alternative minimum tax. And sometimes calculating the size of the payment you owe can be sticky.

ON THE INSTALLMENT PLAN   For a calendar-year taxpayer, estimated tax payments are due to the IRS quarterly:

- April 15
- June 15
- September 15
- January 15

The new tax law includes a major change affecting estimated tax payments—one that may increase the size of the quarterly payments you owe.

Under the old law the total amount of your quarterly installments had to equal the lesser of:

- 80 percent of the tax that will fall due for the return for which you're making the payments (the current year's return); or
- 100 percent of the tax shown on your previous year's return (provided that year's return covered a full year).

The 100-percent test remains unchanged. But the new law increases from 80 percent to 90 percent the proportion of the current year's tax that you must make in estimated tax payments. This change is effective for your first taxable year beginning after December 31, 1986.

To see the effect of this change, suppose that you estimate your current year's tax liability to be $50,000. Last year your taxes totaled $44,000. Under the old law you could make estimated payments based on 80 percent of your current year's liability, which comes to $40,000 ($50,000 times 80 percent). Or you could make the payments based on the full amount of last year's tax liability, $44,000. Obviously you would choose the lesser amount—$40,000.

Your decision would change under the new law, however. Ninety percent of this year's liability comes to $45,000. So, naturally, you would base your quarterly estimated payments on the full amount of last year's liability, $44,000.

Only farmers or fishermen escape this choice. They need to make just one estimated payment to the IRS totaling 66.67

percent of their current year's liability. What's more, they don't have to make that payment until January 15, following the close of the tax year. And if they file their return by March 1 and pay the full balance due at that time, they don't have to make any estimated payments at all.

EXCEPTIONS TO EVERY RULE   The law does excuse people from making estimated tax payments if their tax for the current year, after credit for withheld taxes, is small—that is, less than $500.

It also exempts individuals who owed no tax in the preceding year. To qualify for this exception, however, you must be a U.S. citizen or a resident of the United States for the entire previous year. Also, your last year's tax return must have covered an entire year.

PENALTIES FOR UNDERPAYMENT   What if you underpay your estimated taxes? The penalty you'll owe depends upon the amount of the underpayment and current penalty rates, which are based on interest rates.

As in the past, penalties aren't deductible. And now, neither is money you borrow to pay estimated taxes.

Under the old tax law, as you might fondly recall, you could write off interest payments. So it was often cheaper to borrow the money you needed to make quarterly tax payments than to get hit with the penalty.

Say, for instance, that the penalty rate was 10 percent. If you were in the 50-percent tax bracket, you would have been better off borrowing money and paying deductible interest as high as 19 percent than incurring the 10-percent penalty.

Here's an example: A taxpayer in the 50-percent bracket, you underpay your tax bill by $3000. Say your penalty on the underpayment is 10 percent of that amount, or $300.

If you had borrowed the money to avoid the underpayment penalty at a rate of 17.5 percent, your interest expense would have added up to $525. However, you could have deducted the interest on your tax return and saved yourself $263 in federal taxes. Your net out-of-pocket expense would have been $262—$38 less than the $300 penalty for underpaying your taxes.

Under the new law, however, interest you run up on borrowings used to pay your taxes is considered personal interest. And starting in 1987 your deduction for personal interest will be severely limited. After 1991 it vanishes entirely. (See Chapter 2.)

So after 1990 the only time you'll come out ahead borrowing to avoid the penalty is when interest rates are lower than the penalty you have on the underpayment.

In the example above, for instance, you would be just as well off to incur the penalty rather than borrow to avoid it—unless you could borrow at less than 10 percent.

HOW MUCH HAVE YOU UNDERPAID?   Effective with your first taxable year beginning after December 31, 1986, Uncle Sam considers your quarterly installment underpaid if it falls below 90 percent of your current-year tax liability or 100 percent of last year's. You pay a penalty on the amount your payments fall short. And the sum you've underpaid is figured on a quarterly basis.

Assume that your last year's tax liability was $36,000 and your current-year liability is $180,000. The required estimated payments are the lesser of $9000 (one fourth of $36,000) or $40,500 (one fourth of $162,000, which is 90 percent of $180,000). No fool, you decide to pay $9000 for each of the first three installments.

If you pay at least $9000 for the fourth installment, there's no underpayment—even though your estimated tax payments amount to only 20 percent of your current year's tax liability. Of course, you will have to come up with the $144,000 unpaid balance when you go to file your tax return.

On the other hand, assume that you're short on cash and pay only $5000 for each of the first three installments. You have underpaid each installment by $4000 ($9000 less $5000). And a penalty accumulates on each $4000 underpayment from the date each installment was due.

There are, however, two ways you can reduce or even eliminate the penalty for underpayment once you've incurred it.

Assume, as we just did, that you underpaid each of your first three installments by $4000. If you were to make a final estimated payment of $21,000 ($9000 due on the fourth installment plus the $12,000 in accumulated underpayments from the first three installments), the penalties on those first three installments would stop accruing on the date you make your fourth payment. You would still owe a penalty, but you would have frozen its size on the date of your fourth installment. In this case you would reduce your penalty by approximately $300.

And if you wanted to, you could eliminate the penalty entirely by increasing your withholding toward the end of the tax year. This strategy only works, of course, if you're on salary and subject to withholding.

Here's how you'd use this method. Estimated tax payments that you send directly to Uncle Sam are credited to your account when you make them. Employer withholdings, on the other hand, get different treatment. The government adds up all the income taxes withheld from your wages, salaries, bonuses, pensions, and so on during the year. Then it credits one fourth of the total to each of your quarterly installments. So by having your employer increase your withholding toward the end of the year, you can retroactively atone for underpayments made earlier.

Suppose, for example, that you have substantial income from an investment portfolio, but you pay your estimated tax through payroll withholding. A year-end estimate of your liability reveals that you didn't have your employer withhold enough. It turns out that you have been underpaying your estimated tax at the rate of $5000 per quarter.

At this point even if you were to send Uncle Sam a $20,000 check immediately, you would still owe a penalty. You could, however, have your employer withhold an extra $20,000 from your last salary and bonus check at the end of the year. The government would credit that $20,000 in equal portions back to your earlier quarterly installments. You would owe no penalty at all.

Sometimes, however, you don't want the IRS to credit your withholding equally to all four quarterly installments. Instead you'd prefer to have the amounts withheld credited to the quarter in which they were actually withheld. This tactic could be useful, for instance, if your withholding was greater early in the year.

Let's say you're a retired executive required to pay $10,000 quarterly toward your 1986 estimated tax. Before your retirement on April 1, 1986, your accumulated withholdings from salary, severance pay, and a lottery winning came to $24,000.

Absentmindedly, you make no estimated tax payments during the year. Subsequently you discover you need to make a payment to stop a penalty from accruing. So you make one estimated tax payment—$16,000—on January 15, 1987.

Now, you want to know, how can you minimize your penalty? If you allow the IRS to pro rate your withholding as it normally would, it would credit $6000 ($24,000 divided by four) to each quarterly installment. And the IRS would determine that you had underpaid each of your first three installments by $4000 ($10,000 minus $6000).

But you could claim credit for the amounts withheld on the dates they were actually withheld. In this case the IRS would consider your first two $10,000 installments paid in full. And you would have underpaid the third installment, $6000 ($10,000 times three, minus $24,000).

The second is clearly the better strategy to follow in these circumstances: The penalty on a third-quarter underpayment of $6000 is substantially less than the penalty on a $4000 underpayment in each of the first three quarters.

In order to claim credit for the amounts you had withheld, you should retain proof of the dates of the actual withholding, such as copies of paycheck stubs—in case the IRS should ask.

THE LAST WORD   The law allows the IRS to waive penalties when:

• Your underpayment is due to a disaster, such as a hurricane, or a casualty loss, such as a fire; or
• The underpayment is the result of "reasonable cause," and you had retired after reaching age sixty-two or became disabled in the current or preceding tax year. Unfortunately, the IRS has yet to define "reasonable cause."

Caveat: These waivers are allowed strictly at Uncle Sam's discretion. So they should not be used in planning your estimated payments—only as a last resort.

PART 3

WHAT THE NEW TAX LAW MEANS TO YOUR BUSINESS

CHAPTER 18

AND HERE'S THE GOOD NEWS
Where Business Tax Rates Go from Here—Down

CHANGES AT A GLANCE

Old Law	New Law
Tax rates range from 15 percent to 46 percent	Tax rates range from 15 percent to 34 percent

The new tax rate structure for corporations not only looks like a winner. It is a winner.

Lawmakers slashed the top rate on corporate income from 46 percent to 34 percent.

WHAT GOES UP MUST COME DOWN   Under the old law, corporations paid taxes at these rates:

Taxable Income	Tax Rate (percent)
$25,000 or less	15
$25,001–$50,000	18
$50,001–$75,000	30
$75,001–$100,000	40
Over $100,000	46

There's an additional 5-percent tax on taxable income between $1 million and $1.405 million.

For example, if your corporation reported taxable income of $170,000, your tax bill under the old law would total $57,950. Here's how it adds up:

- 15 percent times the first $25,000, or $3750.
- Plus 18 percent times the next $25,000, or $4500.
- 30 percent times the next $25,000, or $7500.
- 40 percent times the next $25,000, or $10,000.
- 46 percent times $70,000, or $32,200.

Under the new law, when the new reduced rates become fully effective, corporations are taxed at these more favorable rates:

Taxable Income	Tax Rate
	(percent)
$50,000 or less	15
$50,001–$75,000	25
Over $75,000	34

And there's an additional five-percent tax on taxable income between $100,000 and $335,000.

Your company, with its taxable income of $170,000, then, would pay $49,550—or $8400 less—under the new law. The breakdown:

- 15 percent times $50,000, or $7500.
- 25 percent times the next $25,000, or $6250.
- 34 percent times $95,000, or $32,300.
- 5 percent times $70,000, or $3500.

BIGGER ISN'T BETTER   When Congress adopted the Tax Reform Act of 1986, it did small business a big favor. It voted to tax the first $50,000 of corporate taxable income at just 15 percent and the next $25,000 of income at just 25 percent.

But lawmakers didn't want big business to profit.

For example, under the new tax structure a larger company would pocket an extra $11,750 because of the lower rates it would pay on the first $75,000 of corporate taxable income. Too much, the legislators decided. So they included a provision that calls for the lower rates to be gradually phased out once a company's taxable income tops $100,000.

The old law included a similar provision—but the targets were corporations with taxable income in excess of $1 million, not—as in the new law—$100,000. You might say that under the new law, just about any business is big business.

Here's how the system works. An additional 5-percent tax is imposed on every dollar of corporate taxable income between $100,000 and $335,000, for a maximum additional tax of $11,750.

Say your company reports taxable income of $500,000. Its tax liability would add up to $170,000 or:

- 15 percent times $50,000, or $7500.
- Plus 25 percent times $25,000, or $6250.
- Plus 34 percent times $425,000, or $144,500.
- Plus 5 percent times $235,000 (taxable income between $100,000 and $335,000), or $11,750.

The effect of the additional 5-percent tax is to wipe out the benefits of lower rates on the first $75,000 of corporate income. Once a corporation's taxable income tops $335,000, it, in effect, pays a flat tax of 34 percent on all its taxable income.

WAITING GAME   The good news is corporate rates are down. The bad news? You'll have to wait a while to benefit from these lower rates. The new rate structure takes effect for tax years beginning on or after July 1, 1987.

What happens if your company's fiscal year does not end neatly on June 30, 1988, the first full twelve-month period under the new rates? Your company will be subject to a blended rate that will reflect the lower rates for that portion of your corporation's fiscal year that falls after June 30, 1987.

Here's how the new system works in such cases. Say your corporation's fiscal year ends October 31, 1987, and it reports taxable income of $50,000. First, you figure the amount of tax you'd pay if the old rates remained in place for the entire year:

- 15 percent times the first $25,000, or $3750.
- Plus 18 percent times the next $25,000, or $4500.
- For a total of $8250.

Then, you calculate your tax liability as if the new rates were in effect for the entire year:

• 15 percent times your $50,000 of taxable income.
• For a total of $7500.

Next you add up the number of days in your fiscal year that come before July 1, 1987 (in this case, 242), and the number that fall after June 30, 1987 (or 123).

Then you divide the number of days that fall before July 1, 1987 (242), by the number of days in the year (365), to get the percentage of the year's income that is subject to taxation at the old rates—66.33 percent.

You next divide the number of days that fall after June 30, 1987 (123), by 365 to get the percentage of the year's income that is taxed at the new favorable rates—33.67 percent.

Finally, to arrive at your tax bill, you multiply these two percentages times the tax liabilities you calculated earlier:

• 66.33 percent times $8250 (your tax bill, had the old rates remained in place), or $5472.
• 33.67 percent times $7500 (your tax liability, had the new rates kicked in immediately), or $2525.

Add up these sums—$5472 and $2525—and you have, finally, your current tax bill: $7997. The net result: You pay $253 less than you would have under the old law.

But you pay $497 more than you would if the new tax rates had been fully effective, instead of starting on July 1, 1987.

We thought you might want to estimate your corporation's tax bill. So we've included a chart at the end of the chapter showing the marginal tax rates for companies whose fiscal years end on June 30, 1987, through June 30, 1988. These are approximately the same rates you would come up with if you go through the exercise above. The rates are rounded to the nearest one-hundredth of one percent. Also, we've included the blending of the old law and new law 5-percent phase-out tax.

CAPITAL GAINS ON THEIR WAY UP   The new law eliminates the lower 28-percent rate on capital gains. The top rate on capital gains will equal the top corporate rate of 34 percent, once the new lower corporate rates are fully effective—that is, for years beginning on or after July 1, 1987.

In the meantime gains pocketed after 1986 are subject to a top rate of 34 percent, even though the blending of rates for years ending before June 30, 1988, produces a top corporate rate above 34 percent.

Assume XYZ Corporation, a calendar-year corporation, has taxable income of $100,000 for 1987, $10,000 of which is long-term capital gain. Without the 34-percent cap, XYZ's 1987 liability would be $23,987. (See our blended rates table.) However, because the $10,000 capital gain is taxed at a maximum rate of 34 percent, the tax comes to $23,689 (the blended tax rate on $90,000 plus 34 percent on the $10,000 capital gain).

CORPORATE "POCKETBOOK" TAX REDUCED The rate of tax charged on undistributed personal holding company (PHC) income is reduced from the current rate of 50 percent to 28 percent—(38.5 percent for years beginning in 1987)—to reflect the decrease in the individual rates. Computer software companies may be exempt from the PHC tax under the law.

DEFERRED TAXES REDUCED Quite apart from shrinking the amount of tribute due the IRS, the new law's decreased corporate tax rates may well have an attractive by-product—a one-time shot in the arm for many corporate income statements.

Longstanding accounting rules require companies to record two kinds of taxes—current and deferred. The current part is simply the tax liability on this year's tax return. The deferred part arises from items recorded for financial statement purposes in the current period but included in the tax calculation in some future year.

Here's an example demonstrating the effects of the differences in depreciation for book and tax purposes. Say the tax law permits a depreciation deduction in the current year of $1000—but book depreciation is only $400. The difference of $600 is a "timing difference"—that is, it will reverse and become taxable in future years. Under the current accounting rules, the current tax savings—$276 at a 46-percent rate—would be charged for this year's income statement, with an equal amount reported on the balance sheet as "deferred taxes." Under the new law the future tax liability will be $204—assuming a 34-percent rate—

but the $276 stays in the deferred tax account until the timing difference affects the tax calculation—which could be years away.

Many U.S. companies have millions of dollars holed up in their deferred tax accounts—all accumulated over the years at the rates in effect at the time. And that's where the possible income-statement benefit lies.

The present rule that says, "provide at 46 percent, reverse at 46 percent, forget about tax law changes," just may be changed.

In early September the Financial Accounting Standards Board (FASB) released a proposal to change the rules governing accounting for income taxes. Under the proposal, deferred taxes would still be provided but would be calculated under the new rules. Accumulated deferred taxes provided at rates higher than those under the new law would be adjusted downward to the new rates. At the option of the company, the difference would go directly into the income statement in the first year the new accounting rules applied, expected to be as early as 1987.

But don't calculate the jump in pennies per share just yet. The new rules are complex, and there could be offsetting effects. Further, the proposal must survive extensive "due process" procedures before becoming enshrined in the accounting rulebook. There could be changes. Further, despite pleas to accelerate the process, final action on the proposal is not expected before 1987.

THE LAST WORD   Before you spend your anticipated tax savings, however, remember that new rates are only part of the tax reform package. As with everything else in this law, what one hand giveth, the other taketh away. While Congress has decided to push rates down, it has also opted to curtail or eliminate many of the accounting methods, deductions, and credits that businesses have long relied on to reduce their tax liabilities.

The reason: According to estimates prepared by the Joint Committee on Taxation, reducing corporate tax rates spells a loss of federal tax revenues to the tune of almost $117 billion. Since such a shortfall is clearly unacceptable in a "revenue-neutral" reform package, Congress had to look for a new source of funds elsewhere. In the next few chapters we'll take a look at how Congress has made business pay for the slash in overall rates.

BLENDED MARGINAL RATES

| | Taxable Income | | | | | Surcharges | |
Fiscal Year Ending	up to $25,000	$25,001 to $50,000	$50,001 to $75,000	$75,001 to $100,000	over $100,000	Phase-in New Law $100,000 to $335,000 (1)	Phase-out Old Law $1,000,000 to $1,405,000 (2)
Before July 1, 1987	15.00%	18.00%	30.00%	40.00%	46.00%	0.00%	5.00%
July 31, 1987	15.00%	17.75%	29.58%	39.49%	44.98%	0.42%	4.58%
August 31, 1987	15.00%	17.49%	29.15%	39.98%	43.96%	0.85%	4.15%
September 30, 1987	15.00%	17.24%	28.74%	38.49%	42.98%	1.26%	3.74%
October 31, 1987	15.00%	16.99%	28.32%	37.98%	41.96%	1.68%	3.32%
November 30, 1987	15.00%	16.74%	27.90%	37.48%	40.97%	2.10%	2.90%
December 31, 1987	15.00%	16.49%	27.48%	36.98%	39.95%	2.52%	2.48%
January 31, 1988	15.00%	16.23%	27.05%	36.47%	38.93%	2.95%	2.05%
February 29, 1988	15.00%	16.00%	26.67%	36.00%	38.00%	3.33%	1.67%
March 31, 1988	15.00%	15.75%	26.24%	35.49%	36.98%	3.76%	1.24%
April 30, 1988	15.00%	15.50%	25.83%	35.00%	36.00%	4.17%	0.83%
May 31, 1980	15.00%	15.25%	25.41%	34.49%	34.98%	4.59%	0.41%
June 30, 1988 or After	15.00%	15.00%	25.00%	34.00%	34.00%	5.00%	0.00%

(1) Rate is a surcharge in addition to the tax calculated under the taxable income rate. The surcharge rate is applied to the amount of taxable income between $100,000 and $335,000.

(2) Rate is a surcharge in addition to the tax calculated under the taxable income rate. The surcharge rate is applied to the amount of taxable income between $1,000,000 and $1,405,000. This surcharge was in effect under old law and is eliminated as the rates and surcharge under the new law are phased in.

Example:
Taxable income is $1,500,000 and fiscal year end is December 31, 1987.

$0–$25,000	$3,750
$25,001–$50,000	4,123
$50,001–$75,000	6,870
$75,001–100,000	9,245
Over $100,000	559,300
Surcharge (1)	5,922
Surcharge (2)	10,044
Total	$599,254

CHAPTER 19

PICKING UP THE PIECES
Making the Most of Remaining Tax Credits

CHANGES AT A GLANCE

Old Law	New Law
No tax credit is available for low-income housing	The new low-income housing credit equals 9 percent of construction cost, or 4 percent of the acquisition cost of the low-income housing
The rehabilitation credit is 15 percent for buildings at least thirty years old, 20 percent for buildings at least forty years old, and 25 percent for certified historic structures (CHS)	The credit is reduced to 10 percent for non-CHS structures built prior to 1936; 20 percent for CHS
Investment tax credit (ITC) equals 4 to 10 percent of qualifying property	ITC is repealed
Energy credits are available for specified alternative energy projects	Energy credits are initially phased out and then repealed after 1988
The general business credit does not include research activities and low-income housing	The general business credit does include research activities and low-income housing

Congress ruffled more than a few feathers when it decided to do away with a host of popular business tax credits, including the investment tax credit. But it did make a number of people very happy by creating an entirely new tax credit to provide an incentive to builders or rehabilitators of low-income housing.

Here's the lowdown.

SEEKING CREDIT   The new low-income housing credit equals 9 percent of the amount you spend building, or rehabilitating, housing that you rent to low-income people. You subtract the amount of the credit from your tax bill each year for ten years—an overall potential credit of 90 percent! Unlike many other credit provisions, there is no requirement to reduce depreciable basis by the amount of any credit claimed. The credit is limited to 4 percent of the acquisition cost, however, if you opt to purchase existing low-income housing or if you build new housing financed by federal subsidies.

These percentages apply only to projects placed in service in 1987. The law mandates that the Treasury Department set new percentages for these credits each month for property placed in service after 1987.

To claim the credit, your expenditures must exceed $2000 per housing unit. Other requirements:

• At least 20 percent of the housing must be occupied by people whose incomes are 50 percent or less of the median earnings of your community's residents, or at least 40 percent of the housing must be occupied by people whose incomes are 60 percent or less of your community's residents. (Contact your local employment office for statistics on income levels in your community).

• The gross rent paid by families in units that qualify for the credit may not exceed 30 percent of the qualifying income, depending on family size.

• Rental units cannot be used on a transient basis. So hotels, dormitories, hospitals, nursing homes, and so forth do not qualify.

• The housing generally must be available for use after December 31, 1986, and before January 1, 1990.

• The housing must remain as low-income rental property for fifteen years.

YOU'RE NOT GETTING OLDER, YOU'RE GETTING BETTER Congress enacted the rehabilitation credit in 1976 to create an incentive for the real estate industry to preserve historic and other older buildings. Developers received a credit based upon a percentage of the cost they incurred rehabilitating these structures.

Tax reform did not eliminate this credit. But it did modify it.

Under previous law the allowable percentages for computing the amount of the credit you could take on your tax return were:

- 15 percent for nonresidential buildings at least thirty years old.
- 20 percent for nonresidential buildings at least forty years old.
- 25 percent for a Certified Historic Structure. (Check with your local historical society for CHS criteria.)

The new law changes these percentages:

- A CHS now qualifies for a 20-percent credit.
- A 10-percent credit applies to any other building built before 1936.

And as with the old law, you must still meet other requirements before you can claim the credit. The old law demanded that the amount you spent to rehabilitate a building exceed $5000 or the "adjusted-cost basis" of the building, whichever was greater. The adjusted-cost basis was usually the amount you paid for the building less any depreciation you had previously deducted. For example, if you purchased a building for $50,000 and claimed $10,000 of depreciation, your adjusted-cost basis for purposes of the rehabilitation credit was $40,000.

This adjusted-cost basis requirement stands under tax reform. But the new law also says that the adjusted basis you use to calculate future depreciation of all rehabilitated buildings must be reduced by the full amount of the credit you take. And straight-line depreciation must be used for all rehabilitation expenditures added to the original cost of the building.

So if the adjusted-cost basis of a CHS is $40,000, and you spend $100,000 to rehabilitate it, you may claim a credit of $20,000 (20 percent of $100,000). But future depreciation on the building must be computed on an adjusted basis of $120,000 ($40,000 plus $100,000, minus the $20,000 credit).

The law also describes the kinds of rehabilitation that will qualify for the credit. Previously you could claim a credit for the rehabilitation of any building at least thirty years old if you retained 75 percent of the existing external walls in place as external walls. (This rule meant you couldn't place new walls around the old external walls.) The new law keeps that test, but only for a CHS.

Alternatively, under the old law, you could claim the credit if you met the following three tests:

* 50 percent or more of the existing external walls are kept as external walls; and
* 75 percent or more of the existing external walls are kept either as internal or external walls; and
* 75 percent or more of the existing internal structural framework is retained.

The new law requires that you meet these three more rigorous tests for all buildings other than a CHS. This mandatory internal framework requirement means that a non-CHS building can no longer be completely gutted and still qualify for the credit.

These modifications to the rehabilition credit regulations are generally effective for property placed in service after 1986. There are binding contract exceptions, though, for property put to use before 1994. These rules are similar to those for investment tax credits. See your tax adviser for details.

TAKING CREDIT   Some good news: The new law does provide a break if you are eligible for the rehabilitation and low-income housing credits. The credits from these losses can be used to offset the tax on up to $25,000 of nonpassive income. This is true regardless of whether you actively participate in the operation (see Chapter 7).

This benefit also has a phase-out threshold. It applies to taxpayers reporting adjusted gross income between $200,000 and $250,000 before any passive losses. For taxpayers with AGI in excess of $250,000, rehabilitation and low-income housing credits are fully subject to the passive loss limitation.

LIFE AFTER DEATH OF THE INVESTMENT TAX CREDIT
Enacted to promote investment in machinery and equipment used by businesses, the investment tax credit (ITC) has been a big plus for both companies that manufacture equipment and

those that buy it. It allowed businesses to claim a tax credit of 4 to 10 percent for investing in assets, such as computers, cars, and heavy machinery.

But the new tax law kills the ITC outright, and the credit's demise is retroactive to January 1, 1986.

IN TRANSITION Legislators did, however, write transition rules that allow businesses to claim at least partial credits on investments to which they were already committed when Congress began contemplating reform.

You may still claim an ITC on items that you agreed to purchase under a contract that was binding on December 31, 1985, as long as the item is put to use by prescribed deadlines. The deadline depends on each asset's ''midpoint life''—meaning half its useful life. Here's the rundown:

Midpoint Life	In Service By
Less than five years	July 1, 1986
More than five years but less than seven years	Jan. 1, 1987
More than seven years but less than 20 years	Jan. 1, 1989
Twenty years or more	Jan. 1, 1991

Equipment or machinery that your company constructs for use in the business may still qualify for an ITC if construction began before December 31, 1985. Just be sure that by December 31, 1985, you paid out, or committed to pay out, either $1 million or 5 percent of the cost of the property, whichever is less.

If your building or manufacturing plant is under construction in 1985 but isn't completed until 1986 or after, another set of rules applies.

As long as more than one half of the cost of the building, plus any machinery and equipment to be used in the building, was incurred—or was irrevocably committed to—before January 1, 1986, then all the machinery and equipment will qualify for the credit. The machinery does not need to also meet the ''placed-in-service'' deadlines above. If the costs you incur or commit to before January 1, 1986, are not more than one half of the total cost of the building plus equipment, each piece of equipment must be evaluated separately and the placed-in-service deadlines would apply.

For example, suppose that in 1985 you adopted a plan for the construction of a building for your manufacturing operation. Construction costs add up to $100,000; manufacturing machinery and equipment total $80,000. You committed yourself to the cost of the building under a binding contract dated December 1, 1985, and you began construction December 28, 1985. You didn't order the machinery and equipment until February 1986.

Even though you didn't order the equipment until 1986, it is still eligible for the credit, since at least one half of the cost of the building and the machinery ($90,000) was committed to under a binding contract before December 31, 1985.

Now assume the same facts with one exception: The building costs only $60,000. Since less than one half of the cost of the building and equipment—$70,000—was committed to be incurred by December 31, 1985, you must determine the eligibility of the equipment for the credit on a machine-by-machine basis. And since you purchased none of the equipment before January 1, 1986, none is eligible for the credit.

LESS IS MORE   Any property still eligible for the credit under the transition rules is subject to a further limitation on the amount you may claim. This limit is based on the taxable year in which the credit is allowable.

Any regular ITC that, under the transition rules, is allowable in a taxable year beginning after July 1, 1987, is slashed by a full 35 percent. The 35-percent reduction, however, is phased in with the corporate rate reduction. (See Chapter 18.)

If your taxable year straddles July 1, 1987, then your ITC is only partially slashed, reflecting the reduction for the portion of the taxable year after that date. So a calendar-year taxpayer with transitional credits available at December 31, 1987, will have to reduce the credit by 17.5 percent (six of twelve months in the taxable year remaining after July 1, 1987, times 35 percent). For a fiscal-year taxpayer with a year ending March 31, 1988, the credit is slashed by 26.25 percent (75 percent of 35 percent), and so on. This reduction also applies to ITC carryovers— credits generated in a previous year, but not yet used to reduce your tax liability—that you use in years beginning after July 1, 1986.

The basis of the assets that gave rise to the credit must be reduced by 100 percent of the allowable credit amount. For transitional property placed in service within taxable years beginning in 1986, the basis adjustment would be for the reduced amount of the credit. So for transitional property eligible for a 6.5 percent credit—that is, 65 percent of the 10 percent credit—the basis reduction would also be 6.5 percent, not the unreduced 10 percent.

AT MIDNIGHT   The fact that the elimination of the ITC is retroactive to January 1, 1986, may cause headaches for some businesses that have already filed for a fiscal year that included a period after December 31, 1985. These companies will have to amend their returns.

ESTIMATING THE EFFECT   Understatement of 1986 estimated payments is another problem caused by the retroactive repeal of the investment tax credit. Remember, you calculate your estimated tax by estimating your regular tax liability and subtracting your estimated credits. If you calculated ITC for property put to use in 1986, then your first three estimated payments for your 1986 calendar-year tax liability may be too small.

Congress gave you a break though. No penalty for underpayment of estimated tax will be imposed. This applies on all underpayments where you figured in the credit for property put to use in 1986. So you won't be penalized if your estimated payments were understated because you reduced them for 1986 ITC you thought you would be allowed. In fact, this provision applies to any change made by the new law that increases your tax liability in 1986. Individuals have until April 15, 1987, and corporations until March 15, 1987, to pay their full 1986 income tax liability without incurring a penalty.

POWER PLAY   Back in 1978 Congress enacted energy tax credits that allowed businesses to deduct from their tax bills up to 15 percent of the cost of various alternative energy projects or structures. Solar qualified. So did wind, ocean thermal, and geothermal.

Most of these provisions were scheduled to expire at the end of 1985, but all except the wind energy credit got a last-minute reprieve. The new tax law, however, does phase these credits out.

They are available to taxpayers at reduced amounts in 1986 and 1987. And most are eliminated entirely by the close of 1988. Here's the schedule:

Credit	Amount	Dates
Solar energy	15 percent	1/1/86–12/31/86
	12 percent	1/1/87–12/31/87
	10 percent	1/1/88–12/31/88
Geothermal	15 percent	1/1/86–12/31/86
	10 percent	1/1/87–12/31/88
Oceanthermal	15 percent	1/1/86–12/31/88
Biomass	15 percent	1/1/86–12/31/86
	10 percent	1/1/87–12/31/87

JOBS! JOBS!   The old law allowed companies to claim a targeted jobs credit of 50 percent for first-year wages and 25 percent for second-year wages (up to $6000) paid to individuals the law classified as "disadvantaged"—welfare recipients, for example, or children from low-income families. But the credit was only available for wages paid through the end of 1985.

The new law extends the credit for three years. It is therefore available for wages paid to employees who begin work after December 31, 1985, and before December 31, 1988.

You may now claim the targeted jobs tax credit only for individuals you employ for a minimum of either ninety days or 120 hours. Also, the credit for first-year wages is reduced from 50 percent to 40 percent, and the old 25-percent credit for wages paid in the second year of employment is eliminated altogether.

GIVE ME A BOOST   In 1981 Congress did something nice for companies that were willing to boost their spending for research and development: It permitted them to subtract 25 percent of their "increased" expenditures for new product development from their total federal tax bills. The "increase" is figured by subtracting the average amount spent during the past three years from current R&D expenditures.

For example, assume that you shelled out $150,000 in wages and fringe benefits to three programmers working on the development of a sophisticated word processor. In 1982 your R&D expenses added up to $100,000; in 1983, $115,000; and in 1984, $130,000.

Your three-year average, then, came to $115,000. To figure your credit, you subtract $115,000 from $150,000, to get $35,000. You then multiply that amount by 25 percent to get your credit—in this case, $8750.

The credit has been a boon to companies—particularly those in research-intensive high-technology industries. So, in its Tax Reform Act, Congress extended the credit through 1988. But it reduced the amount of the credit to 20 percent, from 25 percent of qualifying expenditures.

Congress also voted to limit the types of R&D costs you may use to figure your annual research and development expenditures, effective retroactively to taxable years beginning in 1986. The reason: The lawmakers suspected that many business owners were overly generous to themselves when they determined which expenditures qualified for the credit. For example, they may have claimed the cost of running their entire research department, even though only a portion of that department's work was geared toward new-product research.

Before you panic about these changes, note that years before 1986 used in your three-year average do not have to reflect the new rules. Prior-year research expenditures are determined using the definition of ''qualified research'' applicable to the year.

The new tax law clearly defines the types of research expenditures that must be excluded when computing the tax credit. Among the types of expenditures nixed: trial production runs, consumer and efficiency surveys, market research and quality control testing, seasonal design expenditures, and management studies.

In addition the new law provides that research expenditures will only qualify for the credit if the research is technological in nature, is part of an experimentation, and is useful in the development of a new or improved business product, process, formula, invention, etc.

Research is technological in nature only if the process of experimentation relies on principles of physics, engineering, biology, or computer science. For example, economic studies that lead to the development of a new type of variable annuity are not technological in nature. The new law further provides that research relating to style, taste, and cosmetic factors will not qualify for the credit. They don't qualify as a product, process, or invention—they're marketing expenditures.

The act also says that the R&D credit may go toward the costs of developing software for internal use only when certain conditions are met. One criterion: The software must meet a ''high threshold of innovation.''

Why this change? Lawmakers didn't think the credit was ever intended to entice and reward a business to develop its own accounts payable program, for example, especially when a suitable or readily adaptable one was already on the market.

The conditions for claiming a credit for internal software development costs are:

• The software must be truly innovative.
• Its development must involve significant economic risk.
• The software must not be commercially available for use by the business.

In addition the internal software development costs are eligible for the credit only if the software is used in research or in a production process involving research qualifying for the credit. For example, you're entitled to a credit if you develop a new software program to control the robotics used in the manufacture of a new product.

BACK TO BASICS   Congress has also revised the rules that apply to the tax credits a business may claim for the research it finances at a university· or other tax-exempt scientific research institution. Now you may claim a 20-percent credit for the increased expenditures your company makes for basic research over a so-called "fixed expenditure floor." Unlike the changes to the R&D credit, these revisions are effective for years beginning in 1987.

THE LAST WORD   The Tax Reform Act increases the cap on all "general" business credits that you may claim. General business credits used to include only the investment tax credit, targeted jobs tax credit, low-income housing credit, and such credits as the alcohol fuels credit and employee stock ownership credit. The act adds the research activities and low-income housing credits to the list. For tax years beginning after 1985 the ceiling is $25,000 plus 75 percent (down from 85 percent under the old law) of your tax liability in excess of $25,000. For purposes of the general business credit, the investment tax credit is included only after reductions required by the transition rules.

CHAPTER 20

THE BEWILDERING NUMBERS GAME
Understanding the New Depreciation Rules

CHANGES AT A GLANCE

Old Law	New Law
Automobiles are depreciated over three years	Automobiles are depreciated over five years
Most machinery and equipment is depreciated over five years	Most machinery and equipment is depreciated over seven years
Real estate is depreciated over nineteen years	Residential rental property is depreciated over 27.5 years; commercial real estate is depreciated over 31.5 years
Real estate is depreciated using the accelerated method	Real estate is depreciated using the straight-line method
Personal property is depreciated using the 150-percent-declining-balance method (accelerated depreciation)	Personal property is depreciated using the 200-percent-declining-balance method (more rapid accelerated depreciation)

The elimination of the investment tax credit (ITC) is one way Congress is recouping the revenues it lost by reducing corporate rates. Modifications in the depreciation rules is another.

What all this "reform" means to any given business will naturally depend a great deal on how heavily the business planned to use credits and depreciation in the future.

For many service-oriented companies—whose deductions consist primarily of compensation and fringe benefits for employees—the new law may spell real tax relief. The reduction in corporate tax rates may well overcome any negative impact that the loss of the ITC, depreciation revisions, and other corporate tax changes have on these companies.

For those businesses that heavily utilize depreciation (or cost recovery, as it's known in the tax code) and investment credits, higher tax bills may be in the offing. Why? Because the decrease in tax rates probably won't offset the effect of the repeal of the ITC and the new depreciation rules.

The objective of the tax reform depreciation changes is to distribute cost-recovery investment incentives more uniformly over all types of equipment. The new law allows use of a more rapid depreciation method—the 200-percent-double-declining-balance method—for nearly all equipment. The old law mandated the 150-percent-declining-balance method.

The depreciation periods will increase under the new law for most personal property, such as business automobiles. In short, the new law provides an attraction not found under the old law: a more rapid depreciation method for personal property. But this boon is diluted by longer depreciation periods.

What happens to real estate? The new law mandates that residental rental property and commercial real estate be depreciated over longer periods. Also, property must be written off using slower methods of depreciation.

In this chapter we provide a rundown on how Congress has revised the depreciation rules—and assess what the changes mean to your business.

KEEP IT SIMPLE   Under the old law most business assets—automobiles and trucks, machinery, computers, furniture, fixtures, buildings, and so forth—were written off using the Accelerated Cost Recovery System (ACRS). Introduced in 1981, the system was notable for its simplicity and fast write-offs.

The ACRS method allowed you to deduct, or recover, more of the cost of an asset in the first few years of ownership—as compared to later years—hence, the term accelerated.

Assets were assigned to different categories. You simply used

IRS tables to determine how long it would take to recover the cost of the asset and how much to deduct each year.

For example, under the ACRS method, trucks were depreciated over a period as short as three years: You wrote off 25 percent of their cost the first year, 38 percent the second year, and 37 percent the third year, assuming you used the accelerated method.

Again, under the ACRS method, machinery, equipment, and office furniture were written off over a period as short as five years: 15 percent the first year, 22 percent the second year, and 21 percent in years three to five.

WRITE IT OFF, WRITE IT ALL OFF　　The new law maintains the ACRS structure (including the acronym). But it tinkers with the way assets are classified and depreciation figured.

For the most part asset classification is based on asset depreciation range (ADR) class lives—that is, the length of time a given asset is expected to be used in a business.

The ADR class life is used to group personal property into classes under the new law. It is always stated in years—office furniture and fixtures, ten years; general purpose trucks, six years; and so forth. This life is generally longer than the period the respective classes use under the new law.

The new tax package changes most of the cost-recovery periods for personal property—that is, all depreciable business assets other than real estate. For most machinery, equipment, furniture, and fixtures, the write-off period climbs from five to seven years—a hefty 40-percent increase. (A major exception: computers, which remain five-year property.) For automobiles and light trucks, the period jumps from three to five years—a 67-percent increase.

But the news isn't all bad. The lengthened write-off periods are somewhat offset by the increased acceleration method that the new law allows. Most depreciable business assets may now be written off using the 200-percent-declining-balance method rather than the 150-percent-declining method.

The 200-percent-declining-balance method results in depreciation that is twice the straight-line depreciation in the first year the asset is placed in service. In each subsequent year depreciation computed under the 200-percent-declining-balance method becomes progressively smaller, until depreciation figured under the straight-line method exceeds the accelerated depreciation. Then the straight-line method is used to complete depreciating the asset. (The 150-percent-declining-balance method is 1.5 times straight-line depreciation.)

A word, before we continue, about conventions: In computing the depreciation deduction, you have to follow certain rules.

For personal property, a "half-year convention" applies. This convention assumes that the property is depreciable for half of the taxable year it is placed in service, regardless of the date you actually began using it. So the deduction you may take the first year is one half the amount that you'd take for a full year of depreciation.

When you dispose of the property—or in the last year of service life—you get to take the other half year of depreciation. So a "three-year depreciation period" actually means that depreciation deductions are taken over four taxable years.

To protect against misuse of the half-year convention, the new law says you can't use it in a year when you place more than 40 percent of your personal property in service during the last quarter of the year. In this case you'd have to use a mid-quarter convention for all personal property placed in service during the year. This convention treats all personal property as placed in service halfway through the quarter in which the property is actually put to use.

Under the old rules it didn't matter how much property you placed in service in the last quarter. You were still entitled to a full six months' depreciation.

The new law says that if you put more than 40 percent of your personal property in service during the last quarter, you're entitled only to 12.5 percent of the first year's depreciation. The percentage applies only to the property placed in service during the last quarter.

At the same time, this mid-quarter convention allows you to write off 87.5 percent of the first year's depreciation for property placed in service during the first quarter. Since 40 percent of the assets are placed in service in the last quarter, however, this convention will result in less total depreciation than the half-year convention.

Here's an example of the difference between the old ACR depreciation—the 150-percent-declining-balance method over three years—and depreciation under the new law—200-percent-declining-balance method over five years.

You purchase a pickup truck on January 1, 1987, for use in

your construction business. The truck costs $9000 and generates a $1800 write-off for 1987. You figure the write-off like this: Divide $9000 by five years and divide the result by two for the half-year convention. Then multiply by two for the 200-percent-declining-balance method. Using the 150-percent-declining-balance method as prescribed by the tables, depreciation for 1987 would be $2250, which is $9000 times 25 percent.

So under the new law taxpayers must compute depreciation by using formulas rather than using simple tables. And this method will prove far more cumbersome than ACRS.

The new law has more drastic effects when it comes to writing off real estate. In addition to lengthening the recovery time, the law mandates that you must use the less favorable straight-line method.

So changes in the depreciation rules will both help and hurt taxpayers.

STRICTLY PERSONAL   Here's how the new law has re-classified personal property.

The new law puts personal property—both new and used—into six classes. Recovery periods range from three to twenty years. The classifications, and examples of property within each class, are as follows:

• Three-year class—includes small tools used in the manufacture of certain products.
• Five-year class—includes light trucks, automobiles, computer equipment, assets used in R&D, oil and gas drilling, construction, and the manufacture of certain products—for example, chemicals and electronic components.
• Seven-year class—office furniture and fixtures, and most other machinery and equipment.
• Ten-, fifteen-, and twenty-year classes—a limited number of other assets, including land improvements.

The 150-percent-declining-balance method is used for the fifteen- and twenty-year classes. The 200-percent-declining-balance method is used for all others. Here's how the system works. You buy a special tool in the three-year class costing $9000 on May 1, 1987. The tool generates a $3000 depreciation deduction for 1987—that is, $9000 divided by three years, then divided by two for the half-year convention, then multiplied by two again for the 200-percent-declining-balance method.

READ IT AND WEEP   Under the new law you write off residential rental property over a period of 27.5 years using the straight-line method. The accelerated method is no longer available for real estate. (See Chapter 5 for more information on depreciating rental property.)

Nonresidential property—an office building or manufacturing plant, for example—now must be recovered over a period of 31.5 years using the straight-line method.

Under the old law the write-off period was the same for both residential and nonresidential real estate. You could deduct both over a period as short as nineteen years, using either the ACRS or straight-line method.

The straight-line method let you deduct the same amount from one year to the next (except for the first and last year of the building's useful life because of the mid-month convention) until the entire cost was written off.

For both residential rental property and nonresidential real property, a mid-month convention applies. Under the mid-month convention, the depreciation for the first year is based on the number of months the property was in service. The property is treated as having been placed in service in the middle of the month. Real property disposed of is treated as having been disposed of in the middle of the month.

Here's how the new law works with nonresidential property—an office complex or factory, say—used in your company's trade or business. You start using an office building that costs $10 million (excluding the cost of the land) on January 1, 1988. The building does not meet any of the transitional rules.

Under the old system you could have deducted $880,000 ($10 million times 8.8 percent—old law ACRS prescribed table percentage).

Under the new law, you may deduct only $304,233 ($10,000,000 divided by 31.5 years, then divided by twelve months, and then multiplied by 11.5 months for the mid-month convention).

THE SWITCH IS ON   In addition to using the new ACRS classes and depreciation methods, you have two other options when it comes to computing depreciation. You may use the new prescribed recovery periods for personal property, and depreciate the assets under the straight-line method, rather than the 200- or 150-percent-declining-balance method.

Under the second option—the alternative depreciation method—the recovery period is equal to either the property's useful life called for by the ADR system or a prescribed period mandated by the new law. You then use the straight-line method to depreciate the asset. Both these periods are usually longer than under the ACRS system.

Some examples of recovery periods under the second option: five years for automobiles and most trucks, twelve years for personal property without a specific ADR life, ten years for furniture and fixtures, and forty years for real estate.

The alternative method usually doesn't work to your advantage. Take our office building in the example above. Using the alternative method, your write-off would come to $239,583 ($10 million divided by forty years, divided by twelve months, then multiplied by 11.5 months for the mid-month convention), instead of the $304,233 computed under the new ACRS system.

In most cases you'll only use the alternative depreciation method when it is required. For example, you must use it for property financed with tax-exempt bonds, for foreign-use property, and when computing alternative minimum taxable income.

What happens when you use the alternative depreciation method for alternative minimum tax purposes? You may recover the cost of personal property using the 150-percent-declining-balance method rather than a straight-line method, if the straight-line method is not used for regular tax purposes.

STILL MORE CHANGES   The new law further limits the amount you may write off for the cost of a luxury automobile. Now you may—to the extent the auto is used for business—deduct up to $2560 in the first year, $4100 in the second year, $2450 in the third year, and $1475 in each succeeding year. The old law let you write off $3200 the first year and $4800 in each succeeding year.

TIMING IS EVERYTHING   For the most part the new depreciation rules apply to assets placed in service after 1986. However, you may elect early application of the depreciation rules for property placed in service after July 31, 1986.

In addition the Tax Reform Act does include transition rules that allow certain exceptions. For example, you may use the old depreciation rules if the property was constructed, rehabilitated, or acquired under a contract that was binding on March 1, 1986, or earlier.

Another example of transition property will be constructed or rehabilitated property, where the lesser of $1,000,000 or 5 percent of the cost of such property had been incurred or committed to, and construction or rehabilitation had begun by March 1, 1986.

Further, for property to qualify under the transition rules, it must be placed in service by January 1, 1989, if it has an ADR life of less than twenty years, and January 1, 1991, if the ADR life is greater than twenty years or if it's real property, such as residential rental property. Only property with an ADR life greater than seven years will qualify for the transition rules.

THE LAST WORD   Here are some strategies to consider:

• Accelerate your purchases of assets as much as you can before 1987 to take advantage of the old depreciation laws in cases where they are more favorable. For companies in the top rate bracket in 1986, taking a higher depreciation deduction will generate permanent tax savings because of the higher tax rates.

• Elect in some cases early application of the new depreciation rules. For some assets—mainly computer equipment—the recovery period will be the same under the new law as under the old law's ACRS. But it makes more sense to use the new law's rules, since they allow you to use the more favorable 200-percent-declining-balance method.

The one potential problem with the second strategy: the 40-percent rule. If you accelerate purchases and opt to depreciate the property under the new provisions, you may fall victim to the 40-percent rule. In such case, your depreciation deductions on this property would be cut.

CHAPTER 21

THE INCREDIBLE SHRINKING EXPENSE ACCOUNT
Business Goes on a Diet

CHANGES AT A GLANCE

Old Law	New Law
Business meal and entertainment expenses are fully deductible	Business meal and entertainment expenses are 80-percent deductible
Business travel by cruise ship is fully deductible	Deductions for cruise-ship travel are limited to a per diem rate
Travel and meal expenses for attending investment-related seminars are fully deductible	These expenses are no longer deductible

The 1986 Tax Reform Act views business meals and entertainment with a substantially more skeptical eye than the old law.

You may still dine out on the company. But you may want to skip dessert, since, under a big change in the tax law, only 80 percent of your tab is deductible. You may also want to forego a stop at your favorite jazz club, since entertainment, too, is only 80-percent deductible.

Drafters of the new law took the view that business diners and revelers tend to spend more than people who are picking up the

check themselves. In essence, argued the lawmakers, business-
people were living high on the hog at the expense of the
government.

They also assumed that eating out and entertaining on the
company conveys personal benefits to business gourmets and
partygoers. It saves them the expense of nonbusiness meals and
entertainment that they probably would have enjoyed anyway.

Since the lawmakers suspected that a lot of business meals had
little to do with conducting business, they've tightened up these
deductions.

NO FREE LUNCH   Eat fast. Under the Tax Reform Act
you may write off only 80 percent of the cost of business meals
for tax years beginning after December 31, 1986. The same
holds true for those Broadway shows.

And it makes absolutely no difference whether you incur the
expense as entertainment or as part of a business trip away from
home. Nor does it matter how much you spend on any given
item. Food, beverages, taxes, tips, tickets, and cover charges are
all just 80-percent deductible.

Let's say you invite a customer to lunch to discuss a sales
contract. Since you want a happy customer, you pick up the tab.
Under the old law you could write off the full cost of the meal on
your tax return. Both you and your customer benefited: Your
customer got a free lunch, while you got to subtract the cost of
your meal from your business income—something you couldn't
have done if you'd eaten alone. Under the old law you could also
write off the cost of attending a sporting event with your customer or renting a private dining room.

But the party's over: It's just these "personal benefits" that
the new law tries to address, however arbitrarily, by allowing
you to deduct only 80 percent of meal and entertainment costs.

SOME THINGS NEVER CHANGE   Taxi fare or other
transportation to the restaurant is still 100-percent deductible—
just as under the old law.

The reason? Transportation, say the lawmakers, is not part of
the entertainment activity. However, parking at a sports arena is
considered part of an entertainment activity, so it is only 80-percent
deductible.

Another important point: The 80-percent rule doesn't change
employee reimbursement policies. When you take a prospective

buyer out for dinner and a show and pay for the meal and show tickets yourself, you can be reimbursed 100 percent by your employer with no tax consequences—as long as you properly document the expense. Your employer, however, may deduct only 80 percent of the amount you're reimbursed.

There are other exceptions. Most food-and-entertainment-related employee fringe benefits are not subject to the 80-percent rule. These fringes include holiday turkeys and hams given to employees, subsidized cafeterias, and food and entertainment provided at company parties, picnics, or other recreational activities.

Taxable employee benefits, such as vacation packages given to a salesperson for outstanding performance, are exempt from the 80-percent rule. The reason: The value of the award is reported as taxable income to the salesperson.

Other exceptions: Promotional items made available to the general public, such as food samples or tickets to promotional events that are given away with a purchase. Also, you get to deduct the full 100 percent for food or entertainment sold at an event if you charge a fair-market amount for attendance.

The new law also makes an exception for meals served at business gatherings, such as conventions, seminars, or meetings that feature a speaker and where no separate charge is made for food and beverage costs. The law specifies that there must be a minimum of forty attendees, more than half of whom must be traveling away from home.

This exception is short-lived, however. The law says that after December 31, 1988, even these food costs will fall under the 80-percent rule. (But you may still deduct the full cost—food excepted—of the business convention or seminar.)

A final exemption from the 80-percent rule: Charitable sports events.

WHEN THE PURPOSE OF BUSINESS WAS LUNCH   Not only does the new law allow you to deduct just 80 percent of the cost of business meals and entertainment, it also requires that the meals have a direct relationship to the conduct of your business.

The old tax law—though fairly strict about entertainment—was thought to be too liberal when it came to business meals. The person you took to lunch or dinner had to have a business relationship to you. But you didn't have to talk about business before, during, or after the meal.

For example, you and Sally went to college together. Now

you both work with computers and often have business dealings. You head the customer service division of a Silicon Valley computer company. Sally is a data-processing manager with a San Francisco bank that uses the computers your company sells.

So, when you travel to San Francisco for the day, whether for business or pleasure, you and Sally usually have dinner. These dinners give you an opportunity to find out if Sally is satisfied with the service she is receiving from your repair people, and what changes need to be made to improve service.

Because your boss wants Sally to be a happy customer, he has instructed you to pick up all the dinner tabs. You are reimbursed for the expense by your company, which in turn deducts the cost of the meals as an ordinary business expense.

Under the old law you and your chum Sally are eating business meals—even if you discuss nothing but mutual acquaintances. Under the new law, if you and Sally don't discuss business before, after, or during dinner, you probably aren't eating a business meal.

The Tax Reform Act now applies the same standard to a deductible business meal that it always applied to entertainment. In addition, the new law imposes new restrictions on business meals. Specifically, for a meal to qualify as a deductible business expense for tax years beginning after 1986:

• You must—as our example illustrates—have a substantial and bona fide business discussion directly before, during, or after the meal.

• You or your employee must be present at the business meal or it can't be deducted. So if you reserve a table at a business dinner but neither you nor your employee attend the dinner, no deduction is allowed. (An attorney, accountant, or other professional adviser may be treated as an employee if he or she is attending the business dinner as your representative.)

• The meal or beverage cannot be "lavish or extravagant." This condition was used previously by the IRS, but the Tax Reform Act now makes it part of the Internal Revenue Code—meaning law and not simply regulations—on business-meal deductions.

SWEET CHARITY   Under the new law, for tax years beginning after 1986, you may no longer deduct any amount over the price stated on an entertainment ticket. So say good-bye to writing off ticket agent's fees or scalper's charges. In addition the new law limits the "face-amount" deduction under the 80-percent rule. The only exception: amounts paid for tickets to a charitable sports event are not subject to either limitation.

The law defines a charitable sports event as one where all proceeds go to a recognized charitable organization and substantially all the work is performed by volunteers. A word of warning: High school and college sporting events do not qualify as charity events.

Not only are the ticket costs of attending a charity sporting event not limited, but food and beverages costs that are part of a package are not subject to the 80-percent limitation.

THE SPORTING LIFE   Keep in mind another new rule. The deduction for the rental of a skybox for more than one event (in excess of nonluxury seating costs) is phased out one third for tax years beginning in 1987, two thirds in 1988, and fully disallowed in 1989.

Your write-off is phased out by the amount the per-event cost of your luxury seats, say $150, exceeds the cost of a regular seat, say $12. Any deduction you get is also subject to the 80-percent-deductibility limitation on entertainment expenses.

Before the Tax Reform Act one of the major entertainment expenditures you couldn't write off was the purchase of "entertainment facilities"—yachts, hunting lodges, vacation resorts, and purchased skyboxes. However, a taxpayer might have been able to circumvent this rule by leasing a skybox instead of purchasing it. So Congress decided to limit deductions for the costs of leasing a skybox for more than an event by expressly disallowing them.

GO WHERE YOU WANT TO GO, BUT . . .   Don't expect as much help from the IRS in paying for the good time you hope to have. For tax years beginning after 1986, the Tax Reform Act lops off some of the especially nice goodies the old law used to allow.

Luxury cruises—and nonluxury cruises, if there is such an animal—are now subject to a maximum per diem rate on deductibility, even when they take you from one place to another on business.

The new law says you may deduct only the amount that does not exceed twice the highest Federal Government allowance for

U.S. travel by employees of the executive branch. The highest Federal Government allowance is currently $126 a day. However, the cost of attending conventions or seminars on a cruise ship remains subject to their pre-tax-reform limitations.

How does the new law affect you, should you be partial to cruises? Assume that you have legitimate business reasons to go from, say, New York to Miami, so you buy a ticket on a cruise ship that happens to be heading south. As we've seen, according to the new law you may write off only $252 a day (two times $126).

But here's a break: Unless the cruise company charges separately for the meals and entertainment you enjoy while on board, or the expense is otherwise clearly identifiable, the entire price of your cruise—up to the daily limit—is fully deductible and not subject to the 80-percent limitation on meal and entertainment expenses.

Other good news: Travel that you take in order to engage in educational activity remains deductible. But under the new law, travel that is the educational activity is not.

For example, a French history scholar may deduct the cost of flying to Paris to perform archival research if the research qualifies as a deductible education expense. But he may not write off the cost of his tour in the Loire Valley—no matter how helpful it was in enhancing his appreciation of the significance of wines to French culture.

Also, under the act, travel expenses you rack up for a charitable organization are not deductible unless there is no significant element of personal pleasure, recreation, or vacation. If you pay for the travel of unrelated third parties who are participants in the charitable activity, you may deduct those costs.

Your write-off is not disallowed, however, if you're on duty "in a genuine and substantial sense" throughout the trip, even if you should, heaven forbid, enjoy your travels. For example, the expenses of a scout leader supervising children on a camping trip are not subject to this disallowance rule.

Other bad news: The travel and meal expenses of attending investment-related conventions—as contrasted to trade or business conventions—no longer qualify as deductions. However, the attendance fee is deductible if, when combined with other deductions, it exceeds the new 2-percent-of-AGI floor on miscellaneous itemized deductions. (See Chapter 3 for more information on itemized deductions.)

CHAPTER 22

WHEN A HOUSE IS NOT A HOME
Strict New Rules for Writing Off Home Offices

CHANGES AT A GLANCE

Old Law	New Law
An employer may rent a portion of an employee's house for use by the employee as an office, and the employee may claim a home-office deduction	Rental arrangements between employers and employees are disallowed
A home-office deduction may not top a taxpayer's gross income from trade or business	A home-office deduction is limited to net income from the trade or business
	A home-office deduction in excess of net income may be carried forward to future years

Working at home has become increasingly popular in recent years. But taking deductions for home-office expenses has become more and more difficult. The 1986 Tax Reform Act continues this trend. However, it stops short of slamming the door entirely on home-office deductions.

As in the past you may still write off such costs as mortgage interest, real estate taxes, and utilities for that portion of your house you use for an office. You may even claim depreciation. And if you rent, you may deduct part of your rental payments.

Also, as in the past, Uncle Sam requires that your home workspace be used regularly and exclusively for business. You may not, for example, use your bedroom as an office by day and sleeping quarters by night. Finally, the office in your house must still meet one of two tests:

- It must be your principal place of business.
- It must be used to meet with clients, patients, or customers in the normal course of business.

As a rule Uncle Sam won't allow you to write off a home office if you use it merely to monitor your investments. Still another catch: If you are employed by someone else, the office must be maintained for the convenience of your employer.

Say your obstetrics practice is located on the main floor of your New York City townhouse, connected by stairs to the family living quarters. Your townhouse office is your only office, and you see your patients nowhere else. You're entitled to a home-office deduction.

But let's say you maintain another office at the local hospital and see most of your patients there. You use your home office as a convenient and comfortable spot to catch up on your "journal reading," and occasionally to meet with a patient. Your home workspace, in this instance, would not be deductible, because your office at the hospital—not the one in your house—is your principal place of business.

Here's another example. Say you work as a distributor for a software start-up. Your company provides no office space for you, and your boss asks if you can work out of your home.

An accommodating employee, you set aside a small den, which you devote exclusively to such work-related tasks as billing customers and soliciting orders. Since you've set up this office strictly for your employer's convenience, you are entitled to write off its costs. (See Chapter 3 for more information on the new rules governing deductions for employee business expenses.)

SOMETHING OLD, SOMETHING NEW   So what has changed under the new law? In the old days many taxpayers would try to sidestep the strict rules for deducting a home office by leasing a portion of their house to their employer. The employer would then authorize the employee to use that part of the home for conducting business. The employee could take a deduction, and it wouldn't matter if the home office was his or her principal place of business. Nor would any of the other tests apply.

Why not? The write-offs the employees took under these circumstances were not, strictly speaking, for the expenses of maintaining a home office. Rather, their deductions fell under another provision of the law that allowed them to claim expenses for renting out part of their home. As long as they limited their deduction to the rent their boss paid them and charged a reasonable rate, this tactic was perfectly legal.

With the Tax Reform Act Congress nixed this practice. These lease arrangements, said the lawmakers, encouraged abuse on two fronts.

For one, they helped employees circumvent the restrictions on home-office deductions. But even worse, they encouraged employees to set up sham compensation transactions: Part of their salary was paid as rent for which they then claimed deductions.

The new law is crystal clear: You may not write off expenses for a home office if you, an employee, lease a portion of your house to an employer.

LOST CAUSE   The new law also tightens up another controversial loophole. The old law said your home-office deduction could not exceed the gross income you received from the business you conducted from your home. The controversy centered on what constituted "gross income."

According to the IRS, gross income equaled gross revenues less any expenses—other than those required to maintain the home office itself. So you first had to reduce the income you received from your home business by any direct business expenses—phone, secretarial help, and so forth—before writing off such home-office costs as maintenance and depreciation.

Say you sold $3000 worth of paper supplies from your basement. Your expenses added up to $5000—$3000 for your home office and $2000 in direct expenses.

In the eyes of the IRS your gross income came to $1000—sales of $3000 minus nonhome office expenses of $2000. Thus, your office deduction was limited to $1000.

Then the tax court stepped in. The IRS interpretation was too strict, it said. Gross income really meant gross revenues before any reduction for direct expenses.

The effect of this ruling: You could use your home-office expenses to increase—or, in some cases, create—your business loss, which you could then deduct from your other income, such as interest, dividends, or wages from other employment.

Here's how it worked. Fresh out of law school, you decided to set up your practice in your home. Since you used a spare room exclusively for your law business, you were entitled to take a home-office deduction.

In your first year you took in revenues of $10,000. But you also spent $9000 for secretarial help, supplies, photocopying, and other office costs. In addition, you ran up $9000 worth of expenses—depreciation, maintenance, and so on—directly related to maintaining an office in your home.

Under the court's interpretation, you first offset your gross revenues of $10,000 with your $9000 of home-office expenses. Your income: $1000. Then you deducted your other business expenses of $9000, creating a net loss for the year of $8000.

Congress sided with the original IRS stance. You may not, says the new law, use your home-office deduction to reduce your taxable income to less than zero.

So now, in the above example, you must first offset your gross revenues by your direct expenses. Since doing so reduces your income to $1000, you may take only a $1000 home-office deduction for the year.

BRIGHT FUTURE   The lawmakers did provide one ray of sunshine, however. You may carry the disallowed home-office deductions forward to later years and use them to offset future income.

Again, assume you post revenues of $10,000 the first year of your law practice. And, again, assume you had an $8000 home-office deduction that year you couldn't claim.

In your second year your revenues climb to $31,000 but your costs remain unchanged. You shell out $9000 for secretarial help, supplies, photocopies, and so on, and $9000 for your home office.

Your income for the year, then, is $13,000—revenues of $31,000 minus expenses of $18,000. Since your net income—$13,000—is more than the home-office deduction you carried forward—$8000—you may write off the entire $8000.

You subtract $8000 from $13,000 to get $5000—the amount of your income from your law practice that is subject to taxation. Because of the carryforward, the amount of the income on which you pay taxes is cut by more than 50 percent.

THE LAST WORD   Like most of the provisions of the new tax law, the rules governing home-office deductions are effective for tax years beginning after December 31, 1986.

CHAPTER 23

PAYING THE PIPER
A Corporate Alternative Minimum Tax with Bite

When it adopted the 1986 Tax Reform Act, Congress wanted to ensure that every corporation pay at least a minimum amount of tax. So it zapped the old add-on minimum tax and created the alternative minimum tax (AMT). The new system applies to tax years beginning after December 31, 1986.

This new AMT is an entirely separate tax system that a corporate taxpayer must address each year in addition to the regular tax system. It is much more complicated than the old add-on minimum tax and will require more intensive planning.

Why the new system? Congress wanted to counter the perception that corporations were not being taxed on their true income.

The new AMT will now require corporations to treat the difference between income listed on their financial statements and income figured for AMT purposes as an "adjustment" in computing AMT for tax years beginning in 1987, 1988, and 1989. After 1989 the use of book income will be replaced by an earnings and profits approach.

This concept adds tremendous complexity to the AMT process. The AMT will now indirectly tax income that was never subject to income tax previously, such as state and local tax-exempt interest.

There is some good news though. Since most tax preferences only defer tax and do not permanently reduce it, the AMT system now offers a mechanism to enable taxpayers to recoup some of the AMT paid.

UNCLE SAM WANTS YOU   Technically, AMT is defined as the excess of the tentative minimum tax (TMT defined below) over the regular tax. It is a flat tax calculated separately from a corporation's regular tax liability, and is applied to a larger portion of a company's income than the regular tax.

HOW DO YOU FIGURE TMT?   To compute TMT you apply the AMT rate of 20 percent to "alternative minimum taxable income" (AMTI) and reduce the result by AMT credits allowed. To reach AMTI: First take regular taxable income and make "adjustments" to reflect the different AMT treatment of certain items, including the following:

- Depreciation on real and personal property placed in service after 1986. (See "New Concepts," below.)
- Gain on sale of assets (placed in service after 1986) depreciated differently for AMT purposes than for regular tax purposes.
- Long-term contracts entered into after February 28, 1986. (See "New Concepts," below.)
- Certain installment sales after March 1, 1986. (See New Concepts," below.)

Then, increase this amount by items of "tax preference," such as:

- Excess percentage depletion over the tax basis of the property.
- Excess of intangible drilling costs incurred in connection with productive oil and gas wells over net income (now limited to 65 percent rather than 100 percent) from such oil and gas properties (now applicable to all corporations).
- Reserves for losses on bad debts in excess of an amount computed on the basis of actual experience for certain financial institutions.
- Excess of accelerated depreciation over straight-line depreciation on real property and leased personal property (if a personal holding company) placed in service before 1987.
- Interest on certain "private-activity" tax-exempt bonds issued generally after August 7, 1986—that is, bonds where the proceeds are being used by nongovernmental persons such as Industrial Development Bonds used by small businesses for plant and building needs.

• Excess of the value of property contributed to a charitable organization and deducted for regular tax purposes over the basis of such property.

The principal difference between the "adjustments" and "tax preference items" is that an adjustment can either increase or decrease AMT income. A preference item always increases income.

The subtotal of regular taxable income, adjustments, and tax preference items is termed "pre-book alternative minimum taxable income." Added (never subtracted) to this amount is the "business untaxed reported profits"(BURP) adjustment. This item is defined as 50 percent of the amount by which adjusted net book income exceeds pre-book alternative minimum taxable income. (See "New Concepts," below.)

After adding this item to the pre-book alternative minimum taxable income, one final adjustment is made for the different amount of net operating losses (NOLs) for AMT purposes. After this final adjustment, the resulting sum is AMTI.

AMTI is then reduced by a $40,000 standard exemption amount. The exemption amount is reduced, however, by 25 percent of the amount by which AMTI exceeds $150,000.

Once AMTI has been reduced by the exemption amount (if any), multiply it by 20 percent. The resulting product is then reduced by allowable foreign tax credits (subject to the 90-percent TMT limitation) and transitional/carryover investment tax credits (subject to the 25-percent TMT limitation).

This amount equals the TMT. To the extent it exceeds the corporation's regular tax, the excess which is defined as the alternative minimum tax (AMT) must be paid in addition to the regular tax.

NEW CONCEPTS   Depreciation adjustment: Under the new law all real estate and personal property placed in service after 1986 will be depreciated differently for AMT than for regular tax purposes. The depreciation adjustment is the "net" difference between the total ACRS depreciation deduction you claim for regular tax purposes and the total depreciation deduction under the alternative method for AMT purposes for post-1986 depreciable property. (See Chapter 20.) Corporations using the alternative depreciation method for AMT purposes only will have to develop at least three different depreciation systems: one for the books, one for regular tax, and one for AMT.

Long-term contract adjustment: For purposes of computing AMTI, any long-term contract entered into after February 28, 1986, must be accounted for under the percentage-of-completion method. Thus, the new 40 percent PCM method will not be available in computing AMTI. Consistent with the computation of the depreciation adjustment discussed earlier, the revenue and expense recognized by using the percentage-of-completion method for the affected long-term contract is substituted for the revenue and expense recognized for regular tax purposes.

Installment sale adjustment: You must report in full for AMT purposes the income on inventory sales, sales by real estate dealers, and sales of rental real estate and real estate used in a trade or business. The latter applies only where the sales price exceeds $150,000. This provision applies to all of the above sales that take place after March 1, 1986.

BURP adjustment: The BURP adjustment is an item that all corporations will have to address in determining whether AMT is applicable in any one year. It is intended as a safety net to pick up timing and permanent differences between financial statement income and taxable income, which are not covered under the AMT adjustments or tax preferences.

Thus, any provision that reduces taxable income but not financial statement income (such as costs incurred satisfying warranty obligations previously accrued for book purposes)—or increases financial statement income but not taxable income (tax-exempt interest on state and local bonds, for example, or the reversal or downward adjustment of an obsolete inventory reserve that was never recognized for tax purposes)—will increase the BURP adjustment.

Conversely, any item that reduces financial statement income more than taxable income (such as amortization of goodwill), or increases taxable income more than financial statement income (for example, gains recognized on sale/leaseback transactions), will reduce the BURP adjustment, but not below zero.

The BURP adjustment will be operative through tax years beginning in 1989. After 1989 the use of book income is replaced with an earnings and profits (E&P) approach.

The starting point in determining this item is net income or loss from the company's financial statements. Recognizing that not all corporations have financial statements that are audited and reported to the public, the new law provides guidelines on sources companies should use to calculate their net income or loss.

Net income or loss may be obtained from the following in order of priority:

• Financial statements filed with the Securities and Exchange Commission.
• Financial statements certified by a CPA and issued to shareholders or used for credit or any other substantial nontax purposes.
• Financial statements provided to a federal, state, or local government or agency.
• A noncertified report or financial statement sent to shareholders or used for credit or for any other substantial nontax purpose.

If a corporation has none of the above, or only has a report or financial statement mentioned in the last category, an election can be made to treat net income or loss equal to the E&P for the taxable year.

Once net income or loss has been established, certain adjustments will have to be made to conform it to an amount consistent with the determination of taxable income for tax purposes. Once the financial statement net income or loss has been adjusted to reflect these items, it is then compared to the pre-book AMTI (before AMT net operating loss), with 50 percent of the excess being the BURP adjustment.

NET OPERATING LOSS   The final adjustment to regular taxable income in determining AMTI is the replacement of the regular tax net operating loss (NOL) deduction with the AMT NOL deduction. In essence a separate computation of the current year AMT NOL—if any—plus the AMT NOL carryover—if applicable—is necessary. In addition the AMT NOL cannot offset more than 90 percent of AMTI before the NOL deduction.

DEFERRAL PREFERENCES   The adjustments required to convert regular taxable income into AMTI reflect, in a sense, part of the ''good news'' in the new AMT rules. Other good news is the minimum tax credit discussed below. The new law now recognizes that the use of most tax preferences results in only a "deferral" of tax liability—not in a complete and final reduction in the corporation's tax payment. These types of items are now referred to as "deferral preferences."

This approach is referred to as the "netting concept," since the AMT methodology allows both additions and reductions from regular taxable income in determining AMTI.

The concept of tax preferences "deferring" tax is not only present in AMT adjustments, but in all other tax preference items as well, except percentage depletion, appreciated property charitable contribution, and private-activity tax-exempt interest preference items (exclusion preferences). Even the BURP adjustment is considered a deferral preference.

MINIMUM TAX CREDIT   Another new concept introduced to ensure that taxpayers will not altogether lose the benefit of certain tax preferences is the "minimum tax credit" (MTC). It represents the total AMT paid, reduced by the amount of AMT that would have been paid if only exclusion preferences were present.

In other words, MTC is allowed only with respect to AMT arising as a result of deferral preferences. Although this amount cannot be carried back, it is carried forward indefinitely to be used as an offset against future years' regular tax liabilities. The regular tax, however, can only be reduced to an amount equal to the TMT in the respective carryforward year.

OTHER CONSIDERATIONS   The final change that corporations must deal with in addressing the new AMT system is the inclusion of AMT as a tax subject to the estimated tax payments requirements. Since most corporations must pay at least 90 percent of their total tax liability via estimated tax payments or be subject to the nondeductible underpayment penalty, this provision could be most troublesome. AMT is a complex calculation, dependent on the regular tax and book income, and corporations will have to monitor their exposure to the AMT on a quarterly basis to avoid the underpayment penalty.

THE LAST WORD   The AMT, as devised, will tax to a large degree a company's actual income.

The BURP adjustment will force corporate taxpayers reporting earnings to stockholders, creditors, and the others to pay a minimum level of federal income tax on such earnings. Exercise caution, however, when planning: Adjustments that accelerate or defer book income must be in compliance with generally accepted accounting principles.

Corporations that are able to manage the timing of income, deductions, and occurrences of originating and reversing AMT adjustments and preferences will be in the best position to deal with the AMT.

CHAPTER 24

OUT OF THE EMPLOYER'S POCKET
New Rules for Providing Retirement Benefits

CHANGES AT A GLANCE

Old Law	New Law
Employees are vested after ten years of service	Employees vest after five years of service
Employees are entitled to receive full retirement benefits at age sixty-two	Employees are entitled to full retirement benefits at age sixty-five

First came the 1974 Retirement Income Security Act.

Then the 1981 Economic Recovery Tax Act.

Next the 1982 Tax Equity and Fiscal Responsibility Act, the 1984 Tax Reform Act, and the 1985 Retirement Equity Act.

Now we have the 1986 Tax Reform Act.

This new law—like all those that preceded it—contains stiff new rules governing company-sponsored pension and retirement plans. In this chapter we take a look at the latest round of changes.

WHAT A DIFFERENCE A YEAR MAKES   When Congress adopted the 1982 Tax Equity and Fiscal Responsibility Act, it capped at $90,000 the maximum annual benefits a person could receive from a pension plan. It also set age sixty-two as the time when a person was qualified to receive full benefits from a company-sponsored pension plan. If an employee retired before this age, the benefits received were reduced for each year he or she fell under the required age.

The new law leaves the $90,000 benefit ceiling in place. But it boosts to sixty-five the minimum age at which a person is entitled to receive full benefits.

It also calls for the minimum age to increase gradually—as it does under Social Security. So for individuals born before January 1, 1938, the retirement age is sixty-five. For individuals born after December 31, 1937, but before January 1, 1945, the retirement age is sixty-six. And for individuals born after December 31, 1944, the retirement age is sixty-seven.

Tax reform also requires companies to use the same formula as the Social Security Administration to calculate benefits for people under age sixty-five. Let's say your employee retires at age sixty-two. Under the law he or she is entitled to only 80 percent of the Social Security benefits payable at age sixty-five. So now the employee will be entitled to only 80 percent of the company-sponsored pension benefits payable at age sixty-five as well.

Say you're slated to pay Tom Jones $90,000 a year at age sixty-five. Under the rules, he'd receive just $72,000 if he retired at age sixty-two. By retiring three years early, he loses $18,000 a year. And if he retires at a relatively youthful fifty-five, he may be entitled to as little as $40,000 a year in pension benefits.

TIGHT FISTED   As we've seen, when Congress adopted the 1982 Tax Equity and Fiscal Responsibility Act, it capped benefits employees could receive from company pension plans. It also reduced to $30,000 the ceiling on the amount a company could contribute in each employee's behalf to a profit-sharing or other defined contribution plan.

The new Tax Reform Act retains the $30,000 ceiling. But it adds a catch: Every dollar your employee contributes to a plan reduces by a dollar the amount your company may contribute in the employee's behalf.

So if Sally Smith salted away $4000 in your company-sponsored pension plan, you may contribute no more than $26,000 on her behalf. The old law allowed employees to make nondeductible contributions of as much as 6 percent of their salary before the employer's allowable contribution was reduced.

YOU'RE ENTITLED   Vesting, simply stated, is an employee's right to receive money from a pension plan, even if he or she resigns or is fired. An employee becomes vested after a specified number of years on the job, a number that is set by the employer within certain standards established by the government. Two of the more popular types of vesting schedules:

• "Cliff vesting" is an all-or-nothing method that entitles workers to receive full benefits after ten years of employment. Short of ten years, they get nothing.
• "Graded vesting" schedules vary widely. One type is based on the so-called "Rule of 15." It entitles employees to receive 25 percent of their retirement benefits after five years on the job and builds up through annual increments to 50 percent after ten years and 100 percent after fifteen years.

The new law accelerates Cliff vesting schedules from ten years to five years effective starting in 1989. The new law also changes graded vesting schedules. It requires that companies vest workers 20 percent after three years, then 20 percent per year until they are fully vested after seven years.

The new rules mean that more employees will be entitled to receive company-paid pension benefits, increasing a company's overall pension costs. The increase may not be as large, however, if a company opts for five-year cliff vesting. In most companies, studies show, employee turnover occurs before the end of five years.

The new vesting rules do not apply until 1989.

Also, union pension plans may retain ten-year vesting. And companies may adopt shorter vesting schedules if they choose.

OPEN-DOOR POLICY   Under the old law a company pension plan had to cover only 70 percent of all eligible employees older than age twenty-one. If a plan satisfied this test, an employer could cover disproportionate numbers of highly compensated employees and rank-and-file employees. The new law says 70 percent of rank-and-file employees must be covered.

Also, under the old law, a company pension plan had to cover a "fair cross section of employees." For example, a pension plan restricted to employees at a company's headquarters would qualify under the guidelines, because the plan still covered a cross section of employees.

The new law modifies this "fair cross section" provision. It allows a company plan to cover a greater number of highly compensated employees provided it covers at least 70 percent of rank-and-file employees.

SEPARATE BUT EQUAL   Under the old law, partners in partnerships could maintain their own retirement plans, as long as benefits were comparable to the benefits provided to the partnership's employees. These plans were popular in large professional firms, such as lawyers' or architects' offices.

The new law nixes these "individual" pension plans. It requires that pension plans cover at least 40 percent of all employees or a minimum of fifty employees.

SOCIAL SECURITY   The new law lessens a company's ability to take credit for its share of Social Security payroll taxes when setting benefit levels under company pension plans.

A company takes credit for company-paid Social Security by "integrating" its plan with Social Security under formulas approved by the IRS. These formulas reflect the company's contributions toward an employee's Social Security benefits through the company's Social Security taxes.

They also reflect the fact that Social Security benefits are weighted toward the lower paid: As pre-retirement salary increases, the percentage of that salary that is "replaced" by Social Security benefits decreases.

The IRS-approved formulas generally allowed pension plan benefits to increase as a percentage of pay as pay increased. The combination of Social Security (weighted toward the lower paid) and pension benefits (weighted toward the higher paid) was intended to produce "level benefits" (as a percentage of pay) across all salary levels. It was possible, under the IRS formulas, to severely reduce or even eliminate company pension benefits for certain rank-and-file employees, leaving the bulk of pension benefits for executives and other highly-paid employees.

The new law does not eliminate integration with Social Security. But starting in 1989, the IRS formulas will be replaced with "tighter" statutory formulas.

The new rules decrease the extent to which pension benefits

may be weighted toward top executives. Under these new rules, contributions and benefits must be provided on all compensation. The rate at which contributions are provided on compensation up to the wage base—for example, for 1986, the first $42,000—must be at the rate at which contributions are paid on excess compensation.

ESOP FABLES   Companies with Employee Stock Ownership Plans, or ESOP's, profit under the tax laws—including the 1986 Tax Reform Act.

An ESOP is a plan that invests in the stock of the sponsoring company. With a leveraged ESOP, the plan itself borrows money to buy stock from the employer. But the loan is repaid when the employer makes tax-deductible contributions to the ESOP.

The old law allowed companies to deduct dividends paid on stock held by an ESOP—as long as the dividends were passed on to employees participating in the ESOP.

The new law retains this rule and goes one step further. It allows companies to deduct ESOP dividends when the dividends go to repay the stock acquisition loan.

Other changes in the ESOP rules: The old law allows lending institutions to exclude from their taxable incomes 50 percent of the interest they receive from loans made directly to ESOP's. The new law expands this tax break to loans made directly to corporations when the corporation transfers stock valued at the same amount of the loan to an ESOP.

REVERSION OF PENSION PLAN ASSETS   Many corporations are finding their pension plans are performing above expectations. So the plans have more assets than needed to fund employee pensions.

In these situations some employers have terminated their pension plans, setting aside funds to meet the pension liabilities and causing the remaining assets to revert to the corporation. Previously the only consequence to the corporation was that excess assets were taxed as income to the corporation.

Under the new law, in addition to income taxes, the corporation will pay a 10-percent excise tax on the reverted fund assets. One way around the 10-percent excise tax: Transfer the amounts recovered from a terminated pension plan to an ESOP and use the money to purchase ESOP stock. When the corporation transfers stock to the ESOP, it receives the reverted assets tax-free.

THE LAST WORD   The employee benefits changes reduce discrepancies between benefits provided for highly compensated employees and rank-and-file employees. To the employer, putting all employees on an equal footing—in terms of benefits—means higher costs. To control this additional expense, employers may find they must make across-the-board reductions in the level of benefits provided.

CHAPTER 25

YOU CAN COUNT ON IT
The New Inventory Accounting Rules

CHANGES AT A GLANCE

Old Law	New Law
Direct and indirect costs are required to be included in inventory under full absorption costing or included in contract cost for long-term contracts	The amount of indirect costs includable in inventory cost under new uniform capitalization rules is increased; all long-term contract costs are includable in contract cost under extended period long-term contract rules

More indirect costs will be added to inventory under the new law than had to be included under the old law. For example, warehousing costs for finished goods in a distribution center will have to be included in inventory costs under the new law.

Under the old tax law some of these indirect costs could be classified as "period" costs. And you did not have to count them as part of the cost of your inventory. This treatment allowed an earlier tax deduction. The reason: If a cost was not included in inventory—that is, if it was classified as a period cost—it could usually be deducted in the year it was paid or incurred.

WHAT'S NEW?   The Tax Reform Act provides a new set of uniform capitalization rules for those companies that must maintain inventories. And these rules mandate that more indirect costs be included in inventory than did prior law—possibly, more than companies add to inventory under generally accepted accounting principles (GAAP). The result: Deductions for costs that under the old law were period costs, are now deferred until the product is eventually sold.

Here's how the new system works. The law directs the IRS to issue uniform rules for the inclusion in inventory of:

 • All costs incurred in manufacturing or constructing real estate or personal property.
 • All costs incurred in acquiring or holding property for resale to others.

It will take a while for affected companies—chiefly manufacturers, contractors, retailers and wholesalers—to know precisely what costs they must inventory and how they should allocate them to production. Why? The Tax Reform Act directs the IRS to come up with these rules.

So what types of indirect costs will companies be required to inventory? Uncle Sam will pattern the new rules after the regulations for extended-period long-term contracts, meaning those that take more than twenty-four months to complete.

FUTURE SHOCK   The following table represents our best estimate of how the indirect costs allocable to inventory under current law will compare to indirect costs that are likely to be allocable under the new uniform capitalization rules.

The table includes only costs that are treated differently under the new law—that is, they now must be included in inventory. So costs that have always been included in inventory (such as maintenance, utilities, and indirect labor and materials) and costs that generally are not (marketing, advertising, and selling expenses, for example) are not reflected in this table.

LITTLE THINGS COUNT   As you can see from this summary, the number of changes is small. But their impact isn't. In fact, these alterations may well be among the most difficult to implement of all the changes required by the Act.

Perhaps the most sweeping change: Indirect general and administrative costs that directly benefit production must be allocated to, and included in, inventory costs. How do you know if a

Legend for cost categorization:

1 = Cost must be included in inventory
2 = Cost not required to be included in inventory
3 = Cost must follow treatment on financial statements if prepared in accordance with costs ordinarily included in inventory under generally accepted accounting principles

Indirect Cost	**Category**	
	Old Law	New Law
Excess of accelerated tax depreciation and amortization over financial statement depreciation and amortization	2	1
Warehousing costs	2	1
Interest(*)	2	1
Other general and administrative costs incident to taxpayer's activities as a whole (for example, personnel department)	2	1
General and administrative costs incident and necessary to production or operations	3	1
Factory general and administrative costs incident and necessary to production or operations	3	1
Taxes (except income taxes)	3	1
Officer salaries incident to production or operations	3	1
Insurance attributable to production or operations	3	1
Strikes, rework labor, scrap, spoilage incident to production or operations	3	1
Current pension contributions	3	1
Current fringe benefit contributions	3	1

*Only for the construction or manufacture of real estate, property costing more than $1 million and requiring more than one year to construct, and property requiring two or more years to construct or manufacture. Does not apply to real estate or personal property acquired solely for resale.

cost benefits production? If it has a causal relationship to production, it benefits production.

For example, the personnel department hires and maintains records for people who operate the machinery that "causes" production. The personnel department, then, has a "causal" relationship to production.

IT'S RELATED   For many of these general and administrative (G&A) costs, the existence of a causal relationship to production can be established. Allocation of these costs to inventory, however, is a complex task.

Suppose, for example, that your accounting office is in a room in the corner of your plant. Part of your total electric bill is allocated to the accounting department—normally a period expense. But a portion of the bill covers electricity used to power equipment used in the manufacturing process—a cost included in inventory. Moreover, part of the total accounting cost, including electricity, is further allocated to the cost-accounting function—now required to be included in inventory.

The company must use some reasonable method to determine how much of the electricity should be allocated to the accounting office and how much of the accounting service relates to the cost-accounting function, and therefore benefits the product.

Even though the mechanics of the allocation of G&A costs are difficult, the basic principles can be simply stated: If a cost benefits or is incurred by reason of a productive activity, it must be allocated to inventory.

For example, personnel costs of recruiting and hiring employees whose labor cost is allocable to production must be allocated. So, too, must accounting and data processing services relating to cost accounting, accounts payable, and materials handling and warehousing costs.

If a cost does not benefit the product and is not incurred by reason of a productive activity (that is, the cost benefits only overall management and policy functions), it does not need to be allocated to inventory. For example, general business planning and economic analysis and forecasting ordinarily will not require allocation to production activities. Nor would the cost of the tax department.

If a cost is beneficial to both productive and nonproductive activities, then it must be allocated among the activities using a reasonable allocation method consistently applied. And if a cost benefits more than one productive activity, it must be allocated to each of the activities.

As noted above, the IRS is expected to turn to the extended-period long-term contract regulations as a guideline for allocation rules. And these regulations are flexible when it comes to allocating indirect costs: They allow any reasonable method of allocation that is consistent with GAAP. For example, the IRS will likely allow allocations based upon the manufacturing-burden rate method or the standard-cost method.

Further discussion of these allocation methods is beyond the scope of this book. They're complicated, so see your accountant or tax adviser.

Another important change: For the first time ever, retailers and wholesalers will be required to include in inventory the cost of buyers, warehousing, and allocable G&A. But Congress gave some wholesalers and retailers a break.

Some smaller retailers and wholesalers get a reprieve from the new uniform capitalization rules. Those with annual average gross receipts of $10 million or less for the three immediately preceding years are not required to follow the new rules. Also, retailers and wholesalers that do have average annual gross receipts of more than $10 million may elect to use a simplified method of applying the uniform capitalization rules. Once you choose the simplified method, you must stick with it.

In general only four categories of indirect costs can be allocated to inventory under this simplified method:

• Off-site storage and warehousing costs (including rent or depreciation for warehouses, property taxes, insurance, and security costs);
• Purchasing costs (for example, buyers' salaries);
• Handling, processing, assembly, and repackaging costs (including the labor cost to unload goods, but not to load for final shipment to customers);
• Any general and administrative costs benefiting the above functions.

Lawmakers in their conference report provided detailed examples illustrating how the above costs are to be allocated to inventory. You may rely on these examples until the Treasury Department issues final regulations. This means the IRS will not challenge your allocation of those costs to inventory as long as you follow the examples in good faith.

The simplified method also provides detailed examples of how to revalue your LIFO (Last-In First-Out) or FIFO (First-In First-Out) inventory after the additional costs have been allocated. This method is simpler for wholesalers and retailers. Nonetheless, you'll want to check with your tax adviser and have him or her show you just how simple it is.

OVER THE LONG HAUL   Another exception: The rules do not apply to costs incurred in connection with a long-term contract. Instead, costs are to be included in and allocated to the contract based upon the existing extended-period long-term contract rules. And this applies even if the contract period is less than two years. These rules parallel the uniform capitalization rules described above.

The extended-period long-term contract rules require that a greater number of costs be included in the contract cost—(the cost of building jet fighter planes or an office building, for example)—than do the rules for contracts expected to be completed in less than twenty-four months. The new law requires that interest incurred with respect to a long-term contract now also be included in the contract cost. Furthermore, costs incurred under cost-plus or federal contracts must be included in contract costs if they are specifically identified in the contract, or in federal, state, or local law applying to the contract.

The extended-period long-term contract rules will not apply to any contract for the construction or improvement of real estate under certain conditions: The contract must be completed within two years and performed by a taxpayer with average annual gross receipts for the three preceding taxable years of less than $10 million. (Since these are real estate construction contracts, however, interest must still be allocated to and included in the contract cost.)

The rules for long-term contracts are retroactive. They are effective for contracts entered into after February 28, 1986.

ON TIME   The uniform capitalization rules for inventory are effective for years beginning after December 31, 1986. So the cost of all inventory that you sell after this date must reflect the changes in the absorption rules.

Here's where the new rules can get really tricky: They apply to inventories for your first taxable year after December 31, 1986, so inventory on hand at the beginning of the first tax year after this date must be revalued to reflect the greater absorption of production costs. You must, that is, revalue all items on hand as if the new absorption rules had been in effect during all prior periods.

To make matters more complicated, this required revaluation is considered a change in accounting method for tax purposes. The difference between inventory as you originally valued it and the revalued inventory must be included in income over four years.

Here's an example: Cogswell Cogs Inc. had an ending inventory value of $100,000 as of December 31, 1986. Now the company's accountants must revalue for tax purposes. They go back to the records supporting the costs used to manufacture the cogs on hand.

Applying the new rules, they determine that indirect costs totaling $10,000 must be added to the cost of the existing inventory. For example, they must add in warehousing costs for finished goods.

After this revaluation, inventory value comes to $110,000. Since these indirect costs—totaling $10,000—were previously deducted as period costs, they must be added back to Cogswell's taxable income over the next four years—25 percent each year. This prevents Cogswell from taking two deductions: First when they were deducted as period costs prior to the law change, and again as the goods are sold subsequent to the inventory revaluation.

How, you may well wonder, are you going to get all the information necessary to revalue the older items in your inventory? Congress has an answer. The new law directs the IRS to issue regulations that let you estimate the amount your inventory will have to be revalued—if you don't have the data you need to be more specific.

Consider this example. The Werdie Buffalo Rhome Co. uses the FIFO accounting method to value its inventory of branding irons. Werdie last produced its iron model A in 1984. From existing records the company's accountants determine that revaluating the 1984 production for greater absorption of indirect production costs results in a 15-percent increase in inventory value.

A portion of the inventory for iron model A is attributable to 1983 production, but the company does not have sufficient infor-

mation for revaluation for that year. Iron model B was last
produced in 1982, but all of that year's critical revaluation data
was lost during a stampede.

The inventory for all other iron models is attributable to
production in 1984 and 1985. Revaluation for these models using
available company records results in a 10-percent increase in
indirect costs.

The regulations will allow the 15-percent increase for model
iron A, attributable to 1984 costs, to be used to value the 1983
production of model A. And Werdie may use the overall 10-percent
increase for the 1984 and 1985 inventory as an estimate to
revalue the model B inventory.

Simple enough, right? If you use FIFO, revaluation using
reasonable cost estimates may not be all that difficult. (Unless,
of course, you have merchandise on hand which has not been
produced for a number of years, for example, spare parts for
outdated products.)

If, however, you use LIFO to value your inventory—and, in
particular, if you use dollar-value LIFO—then tax reform cre-
ates more of a challenge for your cost accountants.

Remember, under LIFO you always assume that inventory
costs are based on your oldest cost of goods—the most recent
cost of widgets purchased were the costs charged to cost of
goods sold. And since your inventory consists of these oldest
costs, it could prove difficult to assemble the data needed to
revalue goods that are three or more years old.

The lawmakers decided that if you don't have the data you
need to revalue your inventory, you may use the average cost
increase of the three years (for which increments in inventory
have occurred) prior to the effective date.

For example, suppose you adopted LIFO in 1980 and your
corporation uses a calendar year. Your inventory levels have
increased steadily each year but your cost records are only
adequate back to 1984. In order to restate your inventory on
hand at January 1, 1987, you may average the cost increase for
1984, 1985, and 1986, and use this figure to restate years 1980
through 1984.

The use of this average percentage revaluation factor can lead
to distorted inventory values, however. Consider, for example,
that data processing departments, an allocable portion of the
costs of which must be inventoried, are relatively new on the
business scene. The base-year LIFO layer would be allocated

data processing costs using the percentage revaluation when these costs didn't exist in the year the base layer was established.

Suppose ABC Corp. bought a computer and began paying an operator in 1985. Under the method above, using the average percentage increase has the effect of including these costs in the base year—and in the 1984 layer—when in fact no computer, or operator salary, existed in these years.

The regulations will provide that, if you can show that inventory layers for certain years are being increased for costs that didn't exist, then the average revaluation percentage can be reduced to compensate. Also, the mechanics of revaluation get tricky. If you carry inventories, consult with your tax adviser before you begin the revaluation process.

Two more points to consider.

As we've seen, the new absorption rules require more indirect costs to be capitalized for tax purposes than for financial accounting purposes under GAAP. (The most glaring example is the excess of tax over financial statement depreciation.)

Furthermore, many companies treat some of these indirect costs as period costs for financial accounting purposes even though they must be inventoried under the new tax law. As such, differences will result in the value ascribed to inventory for financial reporting and tax purposes. Any attempt to conform financial accounting principles to inventory methods used for tax purposes would have to be justified as preferable under GAAP. The result: Many companies may have to establish two cost-accounting systems—one system to determine inventory values under GAAP, and a second to comply with the tax law.

Second, wholesalers and retailers that are required to abide by the new absorption rules may need new tax cost-accounting systems altogether. Previously these taxpayers—under both GAAP and the old tax law—had to include few indirect costs in inventory. Their inventory expenses consisted primarily of the invoice price of acquiring products for resale—the cost of the clothes, tools, or shoes, etc.—plus transportation and other necessary costs to acquire possession—import costs and duties, for example.

Because of the new law they will have to develop a cost-accounting system to nail down and inventory the indirect costs required under the new absorption rules. The simplified method discussed earlier may lessen this problem. But the use of the simplified approach may also result in the inclusion in inventory of more costs than the regular method. Retailers and wholesalers should consider computing the inventory revaluation both ways—and pick the most advantageous.

So how do you plan around the burdensome capitalization revaluation deadline? Here are a few thoughts.

For companies using LIFO, base-year and early-year layers will increase, and the newly absorbed overhead costs may not be relieved until substantial liquidations occur. Generally you will be better off if you locate your actual records and compute your inventory restatement using actual costs. Resort to the three-year average increase method only if you don't have your actual records.

The inventory restatement is considered a change in accounting method for tax purposes. Where applicable, you may also want to consider a change to the "practical capacity" method of inventory costing. Many of the additional indirect costs required to be capitalized under the new law are fixed, indirect costs (such as insurance). Under the practical capacity method, the portion of fixed, indirect production costs relating to idle or unused capacity will be deductible as period costs. These costs would remain period costs and thus be excluded from the inventory restatement. (For financial accounting purposes, a change to the practical capacity method may require justification as preferable under GAAP.)

If all else fails, start dusting off those old inventory ledgers. If you can be reasonably detailed in applying the new absorption rules, then the revaluation of your inventory is likely to be more realistic.

One point is certain: The new uniform capitalization rules require you to capitalize more of your costs now. For many LIFO companies the new rules will result in a loss of previously taken tax deductions, which are unrecoverable until these companies go out of business.

THE LAST WORD   As we've seen, the LIFO method of inventory accounting can be advantageous during periods of rising costs. Since LIFO matches the costs of the most recent purchases of inventories against sales, when costs are rising you get a higher deduction for cost of goods sold and lower taxable income.

Using LIFO, however, can be very complex. This complexity, coupled with greater administrative costs for complying with the

LIFO rules, has discouraged some smaller taxpayers from using the method in the past.

Under the new law, small businesses—those with average annual gross receipts of $5 million or less—may use a simplified way of determining inventory values under the dollar value LIFO method for tax purposes. The simplified method basically allows the use of established indices and pools published by the Bureau of Labor Standards.

Under the new law the computations required to initially convert your inventory to simplified dollar value LIFO, however, may be extremely complex. Further, for financial reporting purposes, a company using the simplified LIFO method may have to demonstrate that the results obtained are substantially consistent with its actual experience. Check with your accountant or tax adviser before you dive in.

INDEX

DIRECTORY OF EQUITABLE OFFICES
All the agencies below are listed alphabetically by state.

ROBERT J. RUSSELL
Birmingham, Alabama
(205) 328-5740

JOSEPH E. MORRIS, JR.
Mobile, Alabama
(205) 343-7260

WILLIAM M. MEHNER
Anchorage, Alaska
(907) 561-5355

GILBERT F. LAWSON
Phoenix, Arizona
(602) 263-7900

JAMES RODNEY GOFF
Little Rock, Arkansas
(501) 223-6900

GERALD MOLINARI
Fresno, California
(209) 449-9105

DERRY E. BISHOP
SALVADOR M. VARELA
Los Angeles, California
(213) 251-1600

M. MICHAEL ROONEY
San Diego, California
(619) 239-0018

WILLIAM H. TOLSON, JR.
GIBBS W. BROWN
San Francisco, California
(415) 781-6200

PAUL A. CASTAGNA
SIDNEY A. SALL
San Francisco, California
(415) 864-8886

RICHARD R. BONADIO
Santa Ana, California
(714) 835-5330

JOHN C. LESTER
Woodland Hills, California
(818) 703-7800

EDWARD J. FEIMAN
Denver, Colorado
(303) 691-5700

JOSEPH H. MILLER
Milford, Connecticut
(203) 877-6556

ROGER MALHOTRA
White Plains, NY
(914) 694-8900

ALPHONSO A. CARLTON
CLARENCE W. WRIGHT
Washington, D.C.
(202) 371-1133

ROBERT M. FRIEDMAN
Delray Beach, Florida
(305) 272-3553

EDWARD A. CURTIS
Fort Lauderdale, Florida
(305) 772-4300

A.W. CASSIDY
Jacksonville, Florida
(904) 353-5611

FERDINAND PHILLIPS, JR.
JOSE S. SUQUET
Miami, Florida
(305) 661-6201

SIDNEY W. LEVY
Tampa, Florida
(813) 876-3077

GEORGE R. NICHOLSON
Atlanta, Georgia
(404) 321-1200

JERRY R. PASS
Atlanta, Georgia
(404) 588-0000

DAVID H. MOORE
Macon, Georgia
(912) 742-7511

RICHARD B. YUST
Honolulu, Hawaii
(808) 521-4911

LAWRENCE ZUPANCIC
JAMES SCHLESINGER
Chicago, Illinois
(312) 321-4990/4998

CALVIN D. KANTER
Northbrook, Illinois
(312) 291-3010

MARVIN R. ROTTER
Northbrook, Illinois
(312) 498-7100

WARREN H. WOODY
Chicago, Illinois
(312) 321-5200

LESLIE WARNER, JR.
Peoria, Illinois
(309) 674-7143

DANIEL L. GRAY
Springfield, Illinois
(217) 525-1443

CARROLL E. CARSON
Rosemont, Illinois
(312) 698-6610

JOSEPH M. IVCEVICH
WILLIAM B. GREEN
Indianapolis, Indiana
(317) 848-5600

RICHARD G. LUGOWSKI
West Des Moines, Iowa
(515) 225-1141

JAMES C. FRENCH
Overland Park, Kansas
(913) 345-2800

WARREN A. WANDLING
Wichita, Kansas
(316) 263-5761

T. LEWIS HENDRICK
Louisville, Kentucky
(502) 425-5353

DONNIE L. WILSON
New Orleans, Louisiana
(504) 524-8771

E. WADE LIPPARD
Shreveport, Louisiana
(318) 869-1144

DONALD N. HOBLEY
Baltimore, Maryland
(301) 837-3666

SONDRA G. SAIONTZ
Baltimore, Maryland
(301) 653-0940

THOMAS J. KLOSE
Rockville, Maryland
(301) 294-0115

ROBERT A. KRUM
WILLIAM H. WOOD, III
Wellesley, Massachusetts
(617) 237-4500

WILLIAM C. MILLAR
Birmingham, Michigan
(313) 644-9200

RICHARD GILBERTSON
Dearborn, Michigan
(313) 561-9580

DARROLL Z. HOWARD
Saginaw, Michigan
(517) 799-9630

LEETHEL NEAL
Troy, Michigan
(313) 362-4900

JAMES R. STEPHENS
Edina, Minnesota
(612) 831-1123

WILLIAM J. QUINN
STALEY M. GENTRY
St. Paul, Minnesota
(612) 224-2391

CECIL BRUNSON
Jackson, Mississippi
(601) 981-1919

JOHN R. CASSIN
Clayton, Missouri
(314) 889-0501

ROBERT E. NELSON
St. Louis, Missouri
(314) 444-0339

JED M. POWERS
Omaha, Nebraska
(402) 397-2112

RALPH W. PELLECCHIA
Clark, New Jersey
(201) 381-3000

JOHN F. KRAHNERT
Edison, New Jersey
(201) 549-7575

FRED A. FOLCO
Glen Rock, New Jersey
(201) 447-9400

ERWIN L. GOLDMAN
Kenilworth, New Jersey
(201) 245-8110

MORTON ELLIS
Mt. Laurel, New Jersey
(609) 235-8100

MICHAEL E. FITZPATRICK
West Orange, New Jersey
(201) 731-8800

EDGAR ENCISO
Albuquerque, New Mexico
(505) 262-2181

HENRY M. ELLIOT, JR.
JOHN A. GRIECO, JR.
Albany, New York
(518) 434-9873

ROBERT A. PETERSON
Buffalo, New York
(716) 849-0550

CLARENCE M. BUXTON
BERNARD DUHAIME
Farmingdale, New York
(516) 293-1100

LAWRENCE B. SHULMAN
Lake Success, New York
(516) 488-1000 and (718) 631-1000

HOWARD S. STARR
SYDNEY KHEDOURI
New Hyde Park, New York
(516) 365-3300

JOHN A. DONOHUE
JEFFREY C. MAPSTONE
Syracuse, New York
(315) 425-6346

JAMES M. MEYER
New York, New York
(212) 704-3300

RALPH M. SOLOMON
LEONARD BLEETSTEIN
THOMAS S. HENDERSON
New York, New York
(212) 692-5000

FRANCIS X. QUEALLY
New York, New York
(212) 551-9100

JAMES E. OBI
New York, New York
(212) 760-8000

JULIAN C. LIGHT
SUE LOURCEY
New York, New York
(212) 330-7103

GERALD J. CHRISTIE
Charlotte, North Carolina
(704) 365-3523

WILLIAM R. STROUD
Raleigh, North Carolina
(919) 781-9550

TERRY L. STRAIN
Fargo, North Dakota
(701) 237-9422

DAVID S. MEYERS
WILLIAM C. LOHNES
Cincinnati, Ohio
(513) 762-7700

GEORGE B. FRANZ
Cleveland, Ohio
(216) 621-7715

ANTHONY J. SPENA
Mayfield Village, Ohio
(216) 461-1700

GEORGE W. JONES
Oklahoma City, Oklahoma
(405) 840-3311

J. GARY BEAGIN
Portland, Oregon
(503) 222-9471

ROLAND M. HAUSMANN
KENNETH R. ROOT
Bala-Cynwyd, Pennsylvania
(215) 667-6115

DANIEL J. TURLEY
J. MARK MACKEY
Exton, Pennsylvania
(215) 524-0444

GEORGE W. KARR
Philadelphia, Pennsylvania
(215) 636-4000

ROBERT C. HARRIS
THOMAS J. DUDDY, JR.
Pittsburgh, Pennsylvania
(412) 392-2700

MANUEL MERCADO
Hato Rey, Puerto Rico
(809) 753-6767

THOMAS LINTON
Columbia, South Carolina
(803) 254-5466

CHARLES G. FLOYD
Sioux Falls, South Dakota
(605) 336-1570

J. JACKSON HILL, III
Memphis, Tennessee
(901) 767-5100

WILLIAM L. WHITE
Nashville, Tennessee
(615) 254-1131

GEORGE A. SLADKY
Dallas, Texas
(214) 386-8100

W. WILLARD PRATT
Fort Worth, Texas
(817) 335-2020

JACK G. ROBERTS
Houston, Texas
(713) 621-7900

JOHN E. GASCHEN
Lubbock, Texas
(806) 762-8891

LARRY L. MAST
San Antonio, Texas
(512) 696-4040

F. BURTON CASSITY
Salt Lake City, Utah
(801) 364-7751

ROBERT H. HALL, JR.
Richmond, Virginia
(804) 288-1100

JAMES B. GURLEY
Roanoke, Virginia
(703) 982-2611

ROBERT R. SANTOS
Seattle, Washington
(206) 728-2400

RANDALL G. RUMBERG
Charleston, West Virginia
(304) 346-0837

JOSEPH V. FUNDERBURK
Parkersburg, West Virginia
(304) 422-3531

CHARLES J. SNYDER
Green Bay, Wisconsin
(414) 437-8186

THOMAS M. MULTERER
Madison, Wisconsin
(608) 231-3600

JOHN L. ELLISON
Milwaukee, Wisconsin
(414) 276-2000

J. MICHAEL DOHERTY
Cheyenne, Wyoming
(307) 634-5901